Plautus, Titus Maccius

THE MENAECHMI : THE
ORIGINAL OF SHAKE-
SPEARE'S "COMEDY OF
ERRORS": THE LATIN
TEXT TOGETHER WITH
THE ELIZABETHAN
TRANSLATION: EDITED
BY W. H. D. ROUSE,
LITT.D.

[BY WILLIAM WARNER]

CHATTO & WINDUS, PUBLISHERS
LONDON   MDCCCCXII

1317

THE SHAKESPEARE LIBRARY.
GENERAL EDITOR PROFESSOR
I. GOLLANCZ, Litt.D.

NON·SANS·DROICT

Printing Statement:

Due to the very old age and scarcity of this book,
many of the pages may be hard to read due to the
blurring of the original text, possible missing pages,
missing text, dark backgrounds and other issues
beyond our control.

Because this is such an important and rare work, we
believe it is best to reproduce this book regardless of
its original condition.

Thank you for your understanding.

THE MENÆCHMI

MENAECMI.

¶ A pleaſant and fine Con-
ceited Comædie, taken out of the moſt excellent wittie Poet *Plautus:*

*Choſen purpoſely from out the reſt, as leaſt harmfull, and
yet moſt delightfull.*

Written in Engliſh, by *VV. VV.*

LONDON
Printed by Tho. Creede,
and are to be ſold by William Barley, at his
ſhop in Gratious ſtreete.
1595.

INTRODUCTION

Sources of the Menæchmi. The Latin play was taken from a Greek original, as the custom was, and as we are told in the prologue. Nothing is known of this original. Because the Menæchmi came from Sicily, Epicharmus has been guessed as the author ; but there is no ground for this, since the art of Epicharmus seems to have been nearer to buffoonery than to comedy, and this play breathes the very air of the New Comedy. What the prologue says about the *Sicilissare* of his author, is shown by the context to refer to the scene, not the dialect. The title Δίδυμοι, or Δίδυμαι, "Twins," is known amongst the plays of Alexis, Anaxandrides, Antiphanes, Aristophon, Euphron, Menander, and Xenarchus. An attempt has been made to show that Poseidippos (who also wrote a Δίδυμοι) was the author, because Cylindrus here is Erotium's slave or servant, and Athenæus says that Poseidippos alone brings in a slave as cook. This is probably not true, and if it were, it is not certain that Cylindrus here is a slave. It remains then to say that any of the poets above named may have been the author, or some one else.

Translations. The *Menæchmi* was acted in Italian at Ferrara, A.D. 1486 (Ruth, *Gesch. der it. Poesie*, ii. 115), and again in 1501 apparently at Milan (Burchardt, *Cultur der Ren.*, 319). It was also drawn upon by Cardinal Bernard Dovitius for his *Calandria*, and by Cecchi for his *Moglie*. The plays of J. G. Trissino, *I Simillimi* (Venice, 1547), and of Agnolo Firenzuola, *I Lucidi* (Florence, 1549), were also founded upon it. The Spaniard Juan de Timoneda published a version in 1559. Other adaptations exist in French and German, before Shakespeare. After the time of Shakespeare we have Rotrou's *Les Ménechmes* acted in 1632 and Regnard's in 1705, Boursault's *Les Menteurs qui ne mentent pas*, Cailhava's *Les Ménechmes grecs*, and Goldoni's *I Due Gemelli Veneziani*. Further information may be got in Dunlop's *History of Roman Literature*, 185 ff., Teuffel's *Hist.*, i. 137, and Ward's *English Dramatic Literature*, i. 373, with the prefaces of Wagner and Ussing to their editions of the Latin play, and that of Prof. Gollancz to the *Comedy of Errors* (Temple Shakespeare); *cp.* also *Menechmi und Amphitruo im englischen drama bis zur 1661*, by Karl Roeder (Leipzig, 1904).

In English. The episode of *Jack Juggler* (1563) is probably the first representation in English of the favourite "farce of mistaken identity." The oldest English translation, which is here reprinted, was by William Warner, and pub-

lished in 1595; he tells us, however, that it had circulated in
MS. before. Shakespeare may have seen it; but on the other
hand, as the *Comedy of Errors* may be fairly dated 1589-91,
Warner may have seen Shakespeare. The only verbal echo is
found in the *Comedy of Errors*, ii. l. 100, where Adriana says
"poor I am but his stale"; in our translation the Wife
says "He makes me a stale and a laughing-stock to all the
world."

Comparison of the Latin with the Translation.

Warner's translation is largely a free paraphrase; he fre-
quently compresses the original, omitting lines or whole
speeches, or giving a pithy summary of the *cantica* or lyric
parts of the Latin. Occasionally a short speech has been
interjected with good effect: instances will be pointed out in the
notes. It is clear that Warner wrote with an eye on the
stage, and his brisk interchange has often the advantage over
Plautus.

Comparison of the Latin with Shakespeare.

Shakespeare has made the play far more complex by the
addition of new characters, Ægeon, Balthazar, Angelo, the
Abbess, Luciana, and especially the second Dromio. He has
also given a touch of suspense and pathos to the play by the
episode of Ægeon, his plain unvarnished tale, and the risk of
death. This is one of his characteristic touches, the comedy
which is almost a tragedy, of which *Much Ado About Nothing*

is one example, and the *Merchant of Venice* another: the
last, indeed, really includes a tragedy, whether Shakespeare
felt it or not. But the great triumph of the *Comedy of Errors*
is the creation of the two Dromios. This can hardly be said
to make the plot more unlikely. The plot anyhow is im-
possible; and if for fun we allow the convention of two twins
exactly alike in person and dress, let us by all means allow a
second pair, and make our fun threefold. The existence of
the twin Dromios makes it possible to begin the confusion
early, and to keep it up with continual variations as long as
the play lasts. In the Latin there is no confusion before
II. ii., when Cylindrus meets Menæchmus Traveller and
his man; Erotium meets them in the next scene, and in the
third act Peniculus and the maid are confronted with them.
The fourth act works off the result of this confusion on
Menæchmus Citizen, and in V. i.–iii. the Traveller meets
the wife and the father-in-law of the Citizen. The Citizen
then comes in for the effects of these meetings, and finally
the twins meet in the last scene.

Shakespeare, however, is able to begin the fun earlier.
His scenes, counted as the Latin, are three in Act I., five
in Act II., five in Act III., seventeen in Act IV., and
eight in Act V. In the third of these (I. ii.) he brings in
the first confusion, when Antipholus the Traveller (if I may
use the same title) meets Dromio the Citizen's man. After

an interval, while this begins to work on the Citizen, the same two meet again, and are next confronted with the Citizen's wife and her sister.——The third act opens with a scene in which recognition is near, Antipholus the Citizen and his Dromio trying to get into their own house, where the two doubles already are. Then comes a meeting of the sister with the two Travellers, which makes the confusion worse. The first scene of IV. is made brisk by a confusion of the two Dromios, who enter one after the other to Antipholus the Citizen. In the following scenes we have further meetings between the Travellers and Adriana, Luciana, and the Courtezan, and between the Citizens and the same, the puzzlement increasing when one pair goes out and the other immediately comes in. Finally, the plot works up to its climax and the two pairs meet: Ægeon is delivered from death, and finds his wife in the Abbess.

The complexity of Shakespeare's plot is not realized until the two plays have been analyzed. The analysis of the *Menæchmi* discloses that Menæchmus the Citizen does not meet any strangers until the last scene, when he is confronted with his double. Menæchmus the Traveller has seven such meetings (counting each of the important characters as one); the Wife, the Father, and Messenio have two each; Peniculus, Erotium, Cylindrus, and the maid one each. On the other hand: in Shakespeare Antipholus the Citizen has

three such meetings, Antipholus the Traveller twelve;
Dromio the Citizen's man has four, and the other Dromio
eleven (counting the house scene as one) ; Adriana the Wife
has seven; her sister Luciana eight; the Courtezan four;
and Luce one. The proportion of Shakespeare to Plautus
is 50 : 17, or nearly three to one. This was made possible
by the invention of the second Dromio.

THE PRINTER TO THE READERS.

The writer hereof, loving Readers, having divers of this Poet's Comedies Englished, for the use and delight of his private friends, who in Plautus' own words are not able to understand them ; I have prevailed so far with him as to let this one go farther abroad, for a public recreation and delight to all those that affect the diverse sorts of books compiled in this kind, whereof (in my judgement) in harmless mirth and quickness of fine conceit, the most of them come far short of this. And although I found him very loath and unwilling to hazard this to the curious view of envious detraction, being, as he tells me, neither so exactly written, as it may carry any name of a Translation, nor such liberty therein used, as that he would notoriously vary from the Poet's own order ; yet sith it is only a matter of merriment, and the little alteration thereof can breed no detriment of importance, I have over-ruled him so far as to let this be offered to your courteous acceptance, and if you shall applaud his little labour herein, I doubt not but he will endeavour to gratify you with some of the rest, better laboured and more curiously polished.

Farewell.

* Where you find this mark, the Poet's conceit is somewhat altered, by occasion either of the time, the country, or the phrase.

ARGVMENTVM

Mercator Siculus, quoi erant gemini filii,
Ei surrupto altero mors optigit.
Nomen surreptici illi indit qui domist
Avos paternus, facit Menaechmum e Sosicle.
Et is germanum, postquam adolevit, quaeritat
Circum omnis oras.   post Epidamnum devenit:
Hic fuerat alitus ille surrepticius.
Menaechmum omnes civem credunt advenam
Eumque appellant meretrix, uxor et socer.
I se cognoscunt fratres postremo invicem.

THE ARGUMENT

* Two twinborn sons, a Sicil merchant had,
Menechmus one, and Sosicles the other :
The first his father lost a little lad,
The Grandsire named the latter like his brother.
This, grown a man, long travel took to seek
His brother, and to Epidamnum came,
Where th'other dwelt enrich'd, and him so like,
That citizens there take him for the same :
Father, wife, neighbours, each mistaking either,
Much pleasant error, ere they meet together.

PERSONAE

Peniculus Parasitus
Menaechmus I
Menaechmus II (Sosicles) } Adulescentes
Erotium Meretrix
Cylindrus Cocus
Messenio Servus
Ancilla
Matrona
Senex
Medicus

Scaena EPIDAMNI

4

THE PERSONS OF THE PLAY

PENICULUS, A PARASITE
MENECHMUS CITIZEN
MENECHMUS TRAVELLER } YOUNG MEN
EROTIUM, A COURTESAN
CYLINDRUS, A COOK
WIFE OF MENECHMUS CITIZEN
MAID TO EROTIUM
OLD MAN, FATHER OF MENECHMUS' WIFE
PHYSICIAN
SLAVES AND PORTERS

A PLEASANT AND FINE CONCEITED
COMEDY,

CALLED

MENECHMUS,

TAKEN OUT OF THE MOST EXCELLENT

POET PLAUTUS

PROLOGVS

Salutem primum iam a principio propitiam
mihi atque uobis, spectatores, nuntio.
adporto uobis Plautum—lingua, non manu :
quaeso ut benignis accipiatis auribus.
nunc argumentum accipite atque animum aduortite   5
quam potero in uerba conferam paucissuma.
   atque hoc poetae faciunt in comoediis :
omnis res gestas esse Athenis autumant,
quo illud uobis graecum uideatur magis ;
ego nusquam dicam nisi ubi factum dicitur.   10
atque adeo hoc argumentum graecissat, tamen
non atticissat, uerum sicilicissitat.
† huic argumento antelogium hoc fuit † ;
nunc argumentum uobis demensum dabo,
non modio neque trimodio, uerum ipso horreo :   15
tantum ad narrandum argumentum adest benignitas.
   mercator quidam fuit Syracusis senex :
ei sunt nati filii gemini duo,
ita forma simili puerei uti mater sua
non internosse posset quae mammam dabat,   20
neque adeo mater ipsa quae illos pepererat,
(ut quidem ille dixit mihi qui pueros uiderat :
ego illós non uidi, ne quis uostrum censeat).

8

PROLOGUE

[BY A LATER HAND]

Good health first of all I wish to us all here present at this play. I bring you Plautus, not on the hand but on the tongue: whom I beg you to receive with gracious attention. Now hear the plot, and give careful ear, which I will set forth as briefly as I may. Note a habit of the poets in their comedies: they place the scene of all their events in Athens, to make you think it all the more truly Greek: I will never say so when it is the fact. Greek this story is indeed, but not Attic; it is Sicilian. So much by way of preface to my plot; and now for the plot itself, measured not by the bushel or the peck but by the whole barn: see how generous is my measure in telling this tale.

There was a merchant at Syracuse, an old man, who had two twin sons, boys so much alike that the nurse who fostered them could not tell which was which, nay not their own mother who bore them: at least so I have been told by one who saw them. I have not seen them myself, pray do not

9

postquam iam pueri septuennes sunt, pater
onerauit nauim magnam multis mercibus ;   25
imponit geminum álterum in nauim pater,
Tarentum auexit secum ad mercatum simul,
illum reliquit alterum apud matrem domi.
Tarenti ludei forte erant quom illuc uenit.
mortales multi, ut ad ludos, conuenerant :   30
puer aberrauit inter homines a patre.
Epidamniensis quidam ibi mercator fuit,
is puerum tollit auehitque Epidamnium.
pater eius autem postquam puerum perdidit,
animum despondit eaque is aegritudine   35
paucis diebus post Tarenti emortuost.
postquam Syracúsas de ea re rediit nuntius
ad auom puerorum, puerum surruptum alterum
patremque pueri Tarenti | esse emortuom,
immutat nomen auos huïc gemino alteri ;   40
ita illúm dilexit qui surruptust alterum :
illius nomen indit illi qui domi est,
Menaechmo, idem quod alteri nomen fuit ;
et ipsus eodem est auo' uocatus nomine
(propterea illius nomen memini facilius,   45
quia illúm clamore uidi flagitarier)
ne mox erretis, iam nunc praedico prius :
idem est ambobus nomen geminis fratribus.
nunc in Epidamnum pedibus redeundum est mihi,
ut hanc rem uobis examussim disputem.   50

think so. When the boys were seven years óld, the father freighted a large ship with merchandise ; one of the twins he took aboard and sailed away with him to Sicily on trading bent ; the other he left at home with the mother. When he came to Tarentum, it happened that there were games afoot : a crowd of visitors, as usual when there are games ; the boy went astray from his father among the crowd. A merchant of Epidamnum who happened to be there, carried off the boy to Epidamnum. The boy thus gone, his father lost heart, and before many days had past he died of that distress at Tarentum. Now when the news came to the child's grand-father at Syracuse, that one of the twins had been lost and the father was dead in Tarentum, the grandfather changed the name of the other twin, and called him by the same name as the lost one ; so dearly did he love the child that was lost. Thus he gave the lost one's name to the one that stayed at home, Menæchmus, the same name as the other had : and he goes by the same name as the grandfather (I remember his name the more easily, because I was present when he was publicly summoned by his creditors). To make all clear, I say once again, that both the twins had the same name.

Now I must post it again to Epidamnum, that I may tell you the whole tale to a T. If any of you gentlemen has any

si quis quid uestrum Epidamnum curari sibi
uelit, audacter imperato et dicito,
sed ita ut det unde curari id possit sibi.
nam nisi qui argentum dederit, nugas egerit ;
qui dederit, magi' maiores nugas egerit.   55
uerum illuc redeo unde abii atque uno asto in loco.
Epidamniensis ill' quem dudum dixeram,
geminum illum puerum qui surrupuit alterum,
ei liberorum nisi diuitiae nihil erat :
adoptat illum puerum surrupticium   60
sibi filium eique uxorem dotatam dedit,
eumque heredem fecit quom ipse obiit diem.
nam rus ut ibat forte, ut multum pluerat,
ingressus fluuium rapidum ab urbe hau longule,
rapidus raptori pueri subduxit pedes   65
apstraxitque hominem in maxumam malam crucem.
illi diuitiae | euenerunt maxumae.
is illic habitat geminus surrupticius.
nunc ille geminus, qui Syracusis habet,
hodie in Epidamnum uenit cum seruo suo   70
hunc quaeritatum geminum germanum suom.
haec urbs Epidamnus est dum haec agitur fabula :
quando alia agetur aliud fiet oppidum ;
sicut familiae quoque solent mutarier :
modo hic hábitat leno, modo adulescens, modo senex,   75
pauper, mendicus, rex, parasitus, hariolus

*   *   *   *   *   *   *

commission for Epidamnum, let him now declare it boldly, not forgetting to provide the wherewithal. Pay your money, or you'll waste your pains; but if you do pay, you'll waste more. But I return to the place I came from, and then I stand again. The Epidamnian of whom I spoke lately, the man that stole the child, had no children but only wealth : he adopts the child for his own, gives him a wife with a dower, and makes him his heir when he died. As he was going by chance into the country, after heavy rain, in fording a swift river not so very far from the city he was carried off by the stream as he had carried off the child, and there was an end of him. The lad had all his great fortune, and here he lives, the stolen twin. Now the other twin, who lives in Syracuse, has come this day to Epidamnum with his slave, to look for this twin brother of his. This is Epidamnum city while our play goes on ; when another play shall be acted this stage will be another place, just as the companies of actors often change : now we have a pander living here, now a young man, now an old, the poor, the beggar, the prince, the parasite, the charlatan.

ACTVS I

SCAENA I

PENICVLVS.

Pe. Iuuentus nomen fecit Peniculo mihi,
ideo quia mensam quando edo detergeo.
homines captiuos qui catenis uinciunt
et qui fugitiuis seruis indunt compedis,
nimi' stulte faciunt mea quidem sententia.   5
nam hómini misero si ad malum accedit malum,
maior lubido est fugere et facere nequiter.
nam se ex catenis eximunt aliquo modo.
tum compediti ei anum lima praeterunt
aut lapide excutiunt clauom.   nugae sunt eae.   10
quem tu adseruare recte ne aufugiat uoles
esca atque potione uinciri decet.
apud ménsam plenam hómini rostrum deliges ;
dum tu illi quod edit et quod potet praebeas,
suo arbitratu | adfatim cottidie,   15
numquam edepol fugiet, tam etsi capital fecerit,
facile adseruabis, dúm eo uinclo uincies.
ita istaec nimi' lenta uincla sunt escaria :
quam magis extendas tanto astringunt artius.

ACT I

SCENE I

Enter PENICULUS, *a Parasite.*

a little tail, brush, sf divien "penis"

Pen. Peniculus was given me for my name when I was young, because like a broom I swept all clean away, where-soe'er I become—namely, all the victuals which are set before me. Now in my judgement, men that clap iron bolts on such captives as they would keep safe, and tie those servants [5 in chains, who they think will run away, they commit an exceeding great folly: my reason is, these poor wretches, enduring one misery upon another, never cease devising how by wrenching asunder their gyves, or by some subtilty or other, they may escape such cursed bands. If then ye [10 would keep a man without all suspicion of running away from ye, the surest way is to tie him with meat, drink, and ease: let him ever be idle, eat his belly full, and carouse while his skin will hold, and he shall never, I warrant ye, stir a foot. These strings to tie one by the teeth, pass all the bands [15 of iron, steel, or what metal soever, for the more slack and easy ye make them, the faster still they tie the party which is in them. I speak this upon experience of myself, who am

15

nam ego ad Menaechmum hunc ⟨nunc⟩ eo, quo iam diu   20
sum iudicatus ; ultro eo ut me uinciat.
nam illic homo hómines non alit, uerum educat
recreatque : nullus melius medicinam facit.
ita est adulescens ; ipsus escae maxumae,
Cerialis cenas dat, ita mensas exstruit,   25
tantas struices concinnat patinarias :
standumst in lecto si quid de summo petas.
sed mi interuallum iam hos dies multos fuit :
domi domitus sum usque cum careis meis.
nam neque edo neque emo nisi quod est carissumum.   30
id quoque iam, cari qui instruontur deserunt.
nunc ad eum inuiso.   sed aperitur ostium.
Menaechmum eccum ipsum uideo, progreditur foras.

Scaena II

Menaechmvs I.   Penicvlvs.

Men. Ni mala, ni stulta sies, ni indomita inposque animi,
quod uiro esse odio uideas, tute tibi odio habeas.
praeterhac si mihi tale post hunc diem
faxis, faxo foris uidua uisas patrem.
nam quotiens foras ire uolo, me retines, reuocas, rogitas,   5
quó ego eam, quam rem agam, quid negoti geram,
quid petam, quid feram, quid foris egerim.
portitorem domum duxi, ita omnem mihi
rem necesse eloqui est, quidquid egi atque ago.

now going for Menechmus, there willingly to be tied to his
good cheer : he is commonly so exceeding bountiful and [20
liberal in his fare, as no marvel though such guests as myself
be drawn to his table, and tied there in his dishes.   Now
because I have lately been a stranger there, I mean to visit
him at dinner : for my stomach methinks even thrusts me
into the fetters of his dainty fare.   But yonder I see his [25
door open, and himself ready to come forth.   [*Stands aside.*]

Scene II

Enter Menechmus [*the Citizen*] *talking back to his
wife within.*

Men. Cit. If ye were not such a brabbling fool and mad-
brain scold as ye are, ye would never thus cross your husband
in all his actions.—'Tis no matter, let her serve me thus
once more, I'll send her home to her dad with a vengeance.
I can never go forth o' doors, but she asketh me whither [5
I go? what I do? what business? what I fetch? what I
carry? *as though she were a Constable or a Toll-

c

nimium ego te hábui delicatam ; nunc adeo ut facturus dicam.

    quando ego tibi ancillas, penum,   11

lanam, aurum, uestem, purpuram bene praebeo nec quicquam

                         eges,

malo cauebis si sapis, uirum opseruare desines.

atque adeo, ne me nequiquam serues, ob eam industriam   14

hodie ducam scortum ad cenam atque aliquo condicam foras.

Pe. illic homo se uxori simulat male loqui, loquitur mihi ;

nam si foris cenat, profecto mé, haud uxorem, ulciscitur.

Men. euax ! iurgio hercle tandem uxorem abegi ab ianua.

    ubi sunt amatores mariti ? dona quid cessant mihi

    conferre omnes congratulantes quia pugnaui fortiter ?   20

hanc modo uxori intus pallam surrupui, ad scortum fero.

    sic hoc decet, dari facete uerba custodi catae.

    hoc facinus pulchrumst, hoc probumst, hoc lepidumst, hoc

                     factumst fabre :

    meo malo a mala apstuli hoc, ad damnum deferetur.

    auorti praedam ab hostibus nostrum salute socium.   25

Pe. heus adulescens ! ecqua in istac pars inest praeda mihi ?

Men. perii ! in insidias deueni. *Pe.* immo in praesidium, ne

                           time.

Men. quis homo est? *Pe.* ego sum. *Men.* o mea commoditas,

                    o mea opportunitas,

salue. *Pe.* salue. *Men.* quid agis ? *Pe.* teneo dextera

                    genium meum.

Men. non potuisti magi' per tempus mi aduenire quam

                       aduenis.

stock

gatherer. I have pampered her too much : she hath servants
about her, wool, flax, and all things necessary to busy her
withall, yet she watcheth and wondereth whither I go. [10
Well, sith it is so, she shall now have some cause : I mean to
dine this day abroad with a sweet friend of mine.

Pen. [*aside*] Yea, marry, now comes he to the point that
pricks me ; this last speech galls me as much as it would do
his wife. If he dine not at home, I am dressed. [15

Men. Cit. We that have loves abroad and wives at home,
are miserably hampered, yet would every man could tame his
shrew as well as I do mine. I have now filched away a fine
riding cloak of my wife's, which I mean to bestow upon one
that I love better. Nay, if she be so wary and watchful [20
over me, I count it an alms-deed to deceive her.

Pen. [*coming forward*] Come, what share have I in that
same ?

Men. Cit. Out, alas, I am taken !

Pen. True, but by your friend. 25

Men. Cit. What, mine own Peniculus ?

Pen. Yours i'faith, body and goods, if I had any.

Men. Cit. Why, thou hast a body.

Pen. Yea, but neither goods nor good body.

Men. Cit. Thou couldst never come fitter in all thy life. 30

Pe. ita ego soleo : commoditatis omnis articulos scio.　31
Men. uin tu facinus luculentum inspicere.?　*Pe.* quis id coxit
coquos ?
iam sciam, si quid titubatumst, ubi reliquias uidero.
Men. dic mi, enumquam tu uidisti tabulam pictam in pariete
ubi aquila Catameitum raperet aut ubi Venus Adoneum ?　35
Pe. saepe.　sed quid istae picturae ad me attinent ?　*Men.*
age me aspice.
ecquid adsimulo similiter ?　*Pe.* qui istic est órnatus tuos ?
Men. dic hominem lepidissumum esse mé.　*Pe.* ubi essuri
sumus ?
Men. dic modo hoc quod ego te iubeo.　*Pe.* dico : homo
lepidissume.
Men. ecquid audes de tuo istuc addere?　*Pe.* atque　[40
hilarissume.
Men. perge, ⟨perge⟩—*Pe.* non pergo hercle nisi scio qua gratia
litigium tibi est cum uxore, eo mi áps te caueo cautius.
—*Men.* clám uxorem ubi sepulcrum habeamus atque húnc
comburamus diem.
Pe. age sane igitur, quando aequom oras, quam mox in-
cendo rogum ?
dies quidem iam ad umbilicum est dimidiatus mortuos.　45
Men. te morare mihi quom obloquere.　*Pe.* óculum ecfo-
dito per solum
mihi, Menaechme, si ullum uerbum faxo nisi quod iusseris.
Men. concede huc a foribus.　*Pe.* fiat.　*Men.* etiam concede huc.　*Pe.* licet

Pen. Tush, I ever do so to my friends; I know how to come always in the nick. Where dine ye to-day?

Men. Cit. I'll tell thee of a notable prank.

Pen. What, did the cook mar your meat in the dressing? Would I might see the reversion. 35

Men. Cit. Tell me, didst thou see a picture, how Jupiter's eagle snatched away Ganymede, or how Venus stole away Adonis?

Pen. Often, but what care I for shadows? I want substance.

Men. Cit. Look thee here: look not I like such a picture? 40

Pen. O ho, what cloak have ye got here?

Men. Cit. Prithee, say I am now a brave fellow.

Pen. But heark ye, where shall we dine?

Men. Cit. Tush, say as I bid thee, man.

Pen. Out of doubt ye are a fine man. 45

Men. Cit. What! canst add nothing of thine own?

Pen. Ye are a most pleasant gentleman.

Men. Cit. On yet.

Pen. Nay, not a word more, unless ye tell me how you and your wife be fallen out. 50

Men. Cit. Nay, I have a greater secret than that to impart to thee.

Pen. Say your mind.

Men. Cit. Come farther this way from my house.

Pen. So, let me hear. 55

Men. Cit. Nay, farther yet!

Pen I warrant ye, man.

Men. etiam nunc concede audacter ab leonino cauo.   49
Pe. eu edepol! ne tu, ut ego opinor, esses agitator probus.
Men. quidum?   *Pe.* ne te uxor sequatur respectas identidem.
Men. sed quid ais?   *Pe.* egone? id enim quod tu uis, id
                           aio atque id nego.
Men. ecquid tu de odore possis, si quid forte olfeceris,
facere coniecturam   *   ?   *
(*Pe.*)   *   captum sit collegium.   55
Men. agedum odorare hanc quam ego habeo pallam. quid
                         olet? apstines?
Pe. summum olefactare oportet uestimentum muliebre,
nam ex istoc loco spurcatur nasum odore inlutili.
Men. olfacta igitur hinc, Penicule. lepide ut fastidis!
                         Pe. decet.
Men. quid igitur? quid olet? responde.   *Pe.* furtum, [60
                        scortum, prandium.
tibi fuant   *
Men. elocutu's, nam   *   *   *   ⟨prandium.⟩
nunc ad amicam deferetur hanc meretricem Erotium.
mihi, tibi atque illi iubebo iam apparari prandium.   *Pe.* eu!
Men. inde usque ad diurnam stellam crastinam potabimus.   65
Pe. [eu!]
expedite fabulatu's.   iam fores ferio?   *Men.* feri.
uel mane etiam.   *Pe.* mille passum commoratu's cantharum.
Men. placide pulta.   *Pe.* metuis, credo, ne fores Samiae
                        sient.

Men. Cit. Nay, yet farther!

Pen. 'Tis pity ye were not made a waterman to row in
a wherry. 60

Men. Cit. Why?

Pen. Because ye go one way, and look another still, lest
your wife should follow ye. But what's the matter? Is't
not almost dinner time?

Men. Cit. See'st thou this cloak? 65

Pen. Not yet. Well, what of it?

Men. Cit. This same I mean to give to Erotium.

Pen. That's well, but what of all this?

Men. Cit. There I mean to have a delicious dinner prepared for her and me. 70

Pen. And me?

Men. Cit. And thee.

Pen. O sweet word! What, shall I knock presently at
her door?

Men. Cit. Ay, knock. But stay too, Peniculus, let's [75

Men. mane, mane opsecro hercle : eapse eccam exit.   oh !

solem uides

satin ut occaecatust prae huius corporis candoribus ?   71

SCAENA III

EROTIVM.   PENICVLVS.   MENAECHMVS I.

Er. Anime mi, Menaechme, salue.   *Pe.* quid ego ?   *Er.*

extra numerum es mihi.

Pe. idem istuc aliis adscriptiuis fieri ad legionem solet.

Men. ego istic mihi hodie apparari iussi apud te proelium.

Er. hodie id fiet.   *Men.* in eo uterque proelio potabimus ;

uter ibi melior bellator erit inuentus cantharo,   5

tua est legió : adiudicato cúm utro—hánc noctem sies.

ut ego uxorem, mea uoluptas, ubi te aspicio, odi male !

Er. interim nequis quin eiius aliquid indutus sies.

quid hoc est ?   *Men.* induuiae tuae atque uxoris exuuiae,

rosa.

Er. superas facile ut superior sis mihi quam quisquam   [10

qui impetrant.

Pe. meretrix tantisper blanditur, dum illud quod rapiat

uidet ;

nam si amabas, iám oportebat nassum abreptum mordicus.

Men. sustine hoc, Penicule : exuuias facere quas uoui uolo.

Pe. cedo ; sed opsecro hercle, salta sic cum palla postea.

Men. ego saltabo ? sanus hercle non es.   *Pe.* egone an   [15

tu magis ?

not be too rash. Oh, see, she is in good time coming forth.

Pen. Ah, he now looks against the sun, how her beams dazzle his eyes!

Scene III

Enter Erotium.

Erot. What, mine own Menechmus! Welcome, sweetheart.

Pen. And what am I, welcome too?

Erot. You, sir? ye are out of the number of my welcome guests.

*Pen. I am like a voluntary soldier, out of pay.   5

Men. Cit. Erotium, I have determined that here shall be pitched a field this day; we mean to drink for the heavens: and which of us performs the bravest service at his weapon the wine bowl, yourself as captain shall pay him his wages according to his deserts.   10

Erot. Agreed.

Pen. I would we had the weapons, for my valour pricks me to the battle.

Men. Cit. Shall I tell thee, sweet mouse? I never look upon thee, but I am quite out of love with my wife.   15

Erot. Yet ye cannot choose, but ye must still wear something of hers: what's this same?

Men. Cit. This? such a spoil, sweetheart, as I took from her to put on thee.

Erot. Mine own Menechmus, well worthy to be my dear, of all dearest.   21

si non saltas, exue igitur. *Men.* nimio ego hanc periculo
surrupui hodie. meo quidem animo ab Hippolyta sub-
cingulum haud
Hercules aeque magno umquam ápstulit periculo.
cape tibi hanc, quando una uiuis meis morigera moribus.
Er. hoc animo decet animatos esse amatores probos.   20
Pe. qui quidem ad mendicitatem se properent detrudere.
Men. quattuor minis ego emi istanc anno uxori meae.
Pe. quattuor minae perierunt plane, ut ratio redditur.
Men. scin quid uolo ego te accurare? *Er.* scio, curabo
quae uoles.
Men. iube igitur tribu' nobis apud te prandium accurarier 25
atque aliquid scitamentorum de foro opsonarier,
glandionidam suillam, laridum pernonidam,
aut sincipitamenta porcina aut aliquid ad eum modum,
madida quae mi adposita in mensam miluinam suggerant;
atque actutum. *Er.* licet ecastor. *Men.* nos prodimus [30
ad forum.
iám hic nos erimus: dum coquetur, interim potabimus.
Er. quando uis ueni, parata res erit. *Men.* propera modo.
sequere tú.—*Pe.* ego hercle uero te et seruabo et te sequar,
neque hodie ut te perdam meream deorum diuitias mihi.—
Er. euocate intus Culindrum mihi coquom actutum foras. 35

Pen. [*aside*] Now she shows herself in her likeness, when she finds him in the giving vein, she draws close to him.

Men. Cit. I think Hercules got not the garter from Hippolyta so hardly, as I got this from my wife. Take this, and with the same, take my heart. 26

Pen. Thus they must do that are right lovers; especially if they mean to [be] beggars with any speed.

Men. Cit. I bought this same of late for my wife; it stood me, I think, in some ten pound. 30

Pen. There's ten pound bestowed very thriftily.

Men. Cit. But know ye what I would have ye do?

Erot. It shall be done; your dinner shall be ready.

**Men. Cit.* Let a good dinner be made for us three. Hark ye, some oysters, a mary-bone pie or two, some artichoks, and potato roots; let our other dishes be as you please. 37

Erot. You shall, Sir.

Men. Cit. I have a little business in this city; by that time dinner will be prepared. Farewell till then, sweet Erotium: Come, Peniculus. 41

Pen. Nay, I mean to follow ye: I will sooner lese my life than sight of you till this dinner be done.

Exeunt [*Pen. and* Men. Cit.]

Erot. Who's there? Call me Cylindrus the cook hither.

SCAENA IV

EROTIVM.   CYLINDRVS.

Er. Sportulam cape atque argentum. éccos tris nummos
                                                    habes.
Cy. habeo.   *Er.* abi atque opsonium adfer;˙ tribu' uide
                                        quod sit satis :
neque defiat neque supersit.   *Cy.* quoiusmodi hic homines
                                                    erunt ?
Er. ego et Menaechmus et parasitus eiius.   *Cy.* iam isti
                                        <u>sunt decem</u> ;
nam parasitus octo | hominum munus facile fungitur.   5
Er. elocuta sum conuiuas, ceterum cura.   *Cy.* licet.
cocta sunt, iube ire accubitum.   *Er.* redi cito.   *Cy.* iam
                                        ego hic ero.—

ACTVS II

SCAENA I

MENAECHMVS II.   MESSENIO.

Men. Voluptas nullast nauitis, Messenio,
maior meo animo quam quom éx alto procul
terram conspiciunt.   *Mes.* maior, non dicam dolo,
quasi aduéniens terram uideas quae fuerit tua.
sed quaesso, quámobrem nunc Epidamnum uenimus ?   5
an quasi mare omnis circumimus insulas ?

Scene IV.

[*Enter* Cylindrus.] Cylindrus, take this hand-basket, and here, there's ten shillings, is there not?

Cyl. 'Tis so, mistress.

Erot. Buy me of all the daintiest meats ye can get; ye know what I mean: so as three may dine passing well, and yet no more than enough.   6

Cyl. What guests have ye to-day, mistress?

Erot. Here will be Menechmus and his Parasite, and myself.

Cyl. That's ten persons in all.   10

Erot. How many?

Cyl. Ten, for I warrant you that Parasite may stand for eight at his victuals.

Erot. Go, despatch as I bid you, and look ye return with all speed.   15

Cyl. I will have all ready with a trice.   *Exeunt.*

ACT II

Scene I

Enter Menechmus Sosicles [*the Traveller*], Messenio
his servant, and some Sailors.

Men. Tra. Surely, Messenio, I think seafarers never take so comfortable a joy in anything, as when they have been long tossed and turmoiled in the wide seas, they hap at last to ken land.   4

Mess. I'll be sworn I should not be gladder to see a whole country of mine own, than I have been at such a sight. But I pray, wherefore are we now come to Epidamnum? Must we needs go to see every town that we hear of?

Men. fratrem quaesitum geminum germanum meum.
Mes. nam quid modi futurum est illum quaerere?
hic annus sextus est postquam ei rei operam damus.
Histros, Hispanos, Massiliensis, Hilurios,   10
mare superum omne Graeciamque exoticam
orasque Italicas omnis, qua adgreditur mare,
sumu' circumuecti.   sí acum, credo, quaereres
acum inuenisses, sei appareret, iam diu.
hominem inter uiuos quaeritamus mortuom;   15
nam inuenissemus iam diu, sei uiueret.
Men. ergo istuc quaero certum qui faciat mihi,
quei sese deicat scire eum esse emortuom:
operam praeterea numquam sumam quaerere.
uerum aliter uiuos numquam desistam exsequi.   20
ego illum scio quam cordi sit carus meo.
Mes. in scirpo nodum quaeris.   quin nos hinc domum
redimus nisi si historiam scripturi sumus?
Men. dictum facessas, datum edís, caueas malo.
molestus ne sis, non tuo hoc fiet modo.   *Mes.* em!   25
illoc enim uerbo esse me seruom scio.
non potuit paucis plura plane proloquei.
uerum tamen néqueo contineri quin loquar.
audin, Menaechme? quom inspicio marsuppium,
uiaticati hercle admodum aestiue sumus.   30
ne tu hercle, opinor, nisi domum reuorteris,
ubi nihil habebis, geminum dum quaeris, gemes.
nam ita est haec hominum natio: in Epidamnieis

Men. Tra. Till I find my brother, all towns are alike to
me : I must try in all places.   10

Mess. Why then, let's even as long as we live, seek your
brother : six years now have we roamed about thus, Istria,
Hispania, Massilia, Illyria, all the upper sea, all high Greece,
all haven towns in Italy.   I think if we had sought a needle
all this time, we must needs have found it, had it been above
ground.   It cannot be that he is alive ; and to seek a dead
man thus among the living, what folly is it !   17

Men. Tra. Yea, could I but once find any man that could
certainly inform me of his death, I were satisfied ; otherwise
I can never desist seeking.   Little knowest thou, Messenio,
how near my heart it goes.   21

Mess. This is washing of a blackamoor.   Faith, let's go
home, unless ye mean we should write a story of our travel.

Men. Tra. Sirra, no more of these saucy speeches ; I
perceive I must teach ye how to serve me, not to rule me. 25

Mess. Ay, so, now it appears what it is to be a servant.
Well, yet I must speak my conscience.   Do ye hear, sir ?
Faith, I must tell ye one thing, when I look into the lean estate
of your purse, and consider advisedly of your decaying stock,
I hold it very needful to be drawing homeward, lest in [30
looking [for] your brother, we quite lose ourselves.   For this
assure yourself, this town Epidamnum, is a place of outrageous
expenses, exceeding in all riot and lasciviousness : and, I

uoluptárii atque potatores maxumei ;
tum sycophantae et palpatores plurumei   35
in urbe hac habitant ; tum meretrices mulieres
nusquam perhibentur blandiores gentium.
propterea huic urbei nomen Epidamno inditumst,
quia nemo ferme huc sine damno deuortitur.
Men. ego istúc cauebo. cedodum huc mihi marsuppium. 40
Mes. quid eo ueis ?   *Men.* iam aps te metuo de uerbis tuis.
Mes. quid metuis ?   *Men.* ne mihi damnum in Epidamno
                                       duis.

tu magis amator mulierum es, Messenio,
ego autem homo iracundus, animi perditi ;
id utrumque, argentum quando habebo, cauero,   45
ne tu delinquas neue ego irascar tibi.
Mes. cape atque serua. me lubente feceris.

SCAENA II

CYLINDRVS.   MENAECHMVS II.   MESSENIO.

Cy. Bene opsonaui atque ex mea sententia,
bonum anteponam prandium pransoribus.
sed eccúm Menaechmum uideo. uae tergo meo !
prius iam conuiuae ambulant ante ostium
quam ego opsonatu redeo. adibo atque adloquar.   5
Menaechme, salue. *Men.* di te amabunt quisquis ⟨es⟩.
Cy. quisquis   *   *   *   ⟨quis⟩ ego sim ?
Men. non hercle uero. *Cy.* úbi conuiuae ceteri ?

hear, as full of ribalds, parasites, drunkards, catchpoles, cony-
catchers, and sycophants, as it can hold. Then for [35
courtesans, why here's the currentest stamp of them in the
world. Ye must not think here to scape with as light cost
as in other places. The very name shews the nature, no man
comes hither *sine damno.*   39

Men. Tra. Ye say very well indeed : give me my purse
into mine own keeping, because I will so be the safer, *sine
damno.*

Mess. Why, sir?

Men. Tra. Because I fear you will be busy among the
courtesans, and so be cozened of it : then should I take [45
great pains in belabouring your shoulders. So to avoid both
these harms, I'll keep it myself.

Mess. I pray do so, sir ; all the better.

Scene II

Enter Cylindrus.

* *Cyl.* I have tickling gear here i' faith for their dinners.
It grieves me to the heart to think how that cormorant
knave Peniculus must have his share in these dainty morsels.
But what ? Is Menechmus come already, before I could come
from the market ? Menechmus, how do ye, sir ? How haps
it ye come so soon?   6

Men. Tra. God a mercy, my good friend, dost thou
know me?

Cyl. Know ye? no, not I. Where's mouldychaps that
must dine with ye ? A murrain on his manners.   10

Men. quos tu conuiuas quaeris? *Cy.* parasitum tuom.
Men. meum parasitum? *Cy.* certe hic insanust homo.   10
Mes. dixin tibi esse hic sycophantas plurumos?

        *   *   *   *

Men. quem tu parasitum quaeris, adulescens, meum?
Cy. Peniculum. *Mes.* éccum in uidulo saluom fero.
Cy. Menaechme, numero huc aduenis ad prandium.
nunc opsonatu redeo. *Men.* responde mihi,   15
adulescens : quibus hic pretieis porci ueneunt
sacres sinceri? *Cy.* nummeis. *Men.* nummum a me accipe :
iube té piari de mea pecunia.
nam équidem | insanum esse te certo scio,
qui mihi molestu's homini ignoto quisquis es.   20
Cy. Cylindrus ego sum : non nosti nomen meum?
Men. sei tu Cylindrus seu Coriendru's, perieris.
ego te non noui neque nouisse adeo uolo.
Cy. est tibi Menaechmo nomen. *Men.* tantum quod sciam,
pro sano loqueris quom me appellas nomine.   25
sed úbi nouisti mé? *Cy.* ubi ego te nouerim,
qui amicam habes eram meam hanc Erotium?
Men. neque hercle ego habeo neque te quis homo sis scio.
Cy. non scis quis ego sim, qui tibi saepissume
cyathisso apud nos, quando potas? *Mes.* ei mihi,   30
quom nihil est qui illic homini dimminuam caput !
Men. tun cyathissare mihi soles, qui ante hunc diem
Epidamnum numquam uidi neque ueni? *Cy.* negas?
Men. nego hercle uero. *Cy.* non tu in illisce aedibus

Men. Tra. Whom meanest thou, good fellow ?

Cyl. Why Peniculus' worship, that whorson lick-trencher, your parasitical attendant.

Men. Tra. What Peniculus? what attendant? my attendant? Surely this fellow is mad.   15

Mess. [*to* Men. Tra.] Did I not tell ye what cony-catching villains you should find here ?

Cyl. Menechmus, hark ye, sir, ye come too soon back again to dinner ; I am but returned from the market. 19

Men. Tra. Fellow, here, thou shalt have money of me, go get the priest to sacrifice for thee. I know thou art mad, else thou wouldst never use a stranger thus.

Cyl. Alas, sir, Cylindrus was wont to be no stranger to you. Know ye not Cylindrus ?

Men. Tra. Cylindrus, or Coliendrus, or what the devil thou art, I know not, neither do I care to know.   26

Cyl. I know you to be Menechmus.

Men. Tra. Thou shouldst be in thy wits, in that thou namest me so right ; but tell me, where hast thou known me ?

Cyl. Where ? Even here, where ye first fell in love with my mistress Erotium.   31

Men. Tra. I neither have lover, neither know I who thou art.

Cyl. Know ye not who I am, who fills your cup and dresses your meat at our house ?

Mess. What a slave is this ! that I had somewhat to break the rascal's pate withal.   36

Men. Tra. At your house, when as I never came in Epidamnum till this day ?

Cyl. Oh, that's true ! Do ye not dwell in yonder house? 39

habitas ? *Men.* di illos homines qui illi[c] habitant perduint !
Cy. insanit hicquidem, qui ipse male dicit sibi.   36
audin, Menaechme ? *Men.* quid uis ? *Cy.* si me consulas,
nummum illum quem mihi dudum pollicitu's dare
(nam tu quidem hercle certo non sanu's satis,
Menaechme, qui nunc ipsus male dicas tibi)   40
ubeas, si sapias, porculum adferri tibi.
Mes. eu hercle hóminem multum et odiosum mihi !
Cy. solet iocari saepe mecum illoc modo.
quam uis ridiculus est, ubi uxor non adest.
quid ais tu ? quid ais, inquam. satin hoc quod uides 45
tribu' uobis opsonatumst, an opsono amplius,
tibi et parasito et mulieri ? *Men.* quas [tu] mulieres,
quos tu parasitos loquere ? *Mes.* quod te urget scelus
qui huic sis molestus ? *Cy.* quid tibi mecum est rei ?
ego te non noui : cum hoc quem noui fabulor.   50
Mes. non edepol tú homo sanus es, certo scio.
Cy. iam ergo haec madebunt faxo, nil morabitur.
proin tu ne quo abeas longius ab aedibus.
numquid uis ? *Men.* ut eas maxumam malam crucem.
Cy. ire hercle meliust te—interim atque accumbere, 55
dum ego haec appono ad Volcani uiolentiam.
ibo intro et dicam te hic astare Erotio,
ut te hinc abducat potius quam hic astes foris.—
Men. iamne abiit ? ⟨abiit⟩. edepol hau mendacia
tua uerba experior esse. *Mes.* opseruato modo : 60
nam istic meretricem credo habitare mulierem,

Men. Tra. Foul shame light upon them that dwell there, for my part.

Cyl. Questionless, he is mad indeed, to curse himself thus. Hark ye, Menechmus!

Men. Tra. What say'st thou? 44

Cyl. If I may advise ye, ye shall bestow this money which ye offered me, upon a sacrifice for yourself; for out of doubt you are mad, that curse yourself.

Mess. What a varlet art thou to trouble us thus!

Cyl. Tush, he will many times jest with me thus. Yet when his wife is not by, 'tis a ridiculous jest. 50

Men. Tra. What's that?

Cyl. This I say. Think ye I have brought meat enough for three of you? If not, I'll fetch more for you and your wench, and Snatchcrust, your Parasite.

Men. Tra. What wenches? What Parasites? 55

Mess. Villain, I'll make thee tell me what thou meanest by all this talk.

Cyl. [*to* Mess.] Away, Jack Napes; I say nothing to thee, for I know thee not: I speak to him that I know.

Men. Tra. Out, drunken fool, without doubt thou art out of thy wits. 61

Cyl. That you shall see by the dressing of your meat. Go, go, ye were better to go in and find somewhat to do there, whiles your dinner is making ready. I'll tell my mistress ye be here. [*Exit.*] 65

Men. Tra. Is he gone? Messenio, I think upon thy words already.

Mess. Tush, mark, I pray. I'll lay forty pound here dwells some courtesan to whom this fellow belongs.

ut quidem ille insanus dixit qui hinc abiit modo.
Men. sed miror quí ille nouerit nomen meum.
Mes. minime hercle mirum.   morem hunc meretrices habent:
ad portum mittunt seruolos, ancillulas ;   65
sei qua peregrina nauis in portum aduenit,
rogitant quoiatis sit, quid ei nomen siet
postilla extemplo se adplicant, adglutinant :
si pellexerunt, perditum amittunt domum.
nunc in istoc portu stat nauis praedatoria,   70
aps qua cauendum nobis sane censeo.
Men. mones quidem hercle recte.   *Mes.* tum demum sciam
recte monuisse, si tu recte caueris.
Men. tacedum parumper, nam concrepuit ostium :
uideamus qui hinc egreditur.   *Mes.* hoc ponam interim.   75
adseruatote haec sultis, nauales pedes.

SCAENA III

EROTIVM.   MENAECHMVS II.   MESSENIO.

Er.   Sine fores sic, abi, nolo operiri.
            intus para, cura, uide, quod opust fiat :
         sternite lectos, incendite odores ; munditia
            inlecebra animost amantium.
         amanti amoenitas malost, nobis lucrost.   5
sed ubi ille est quem coquos ante aedis esse ait ? atque eccum
                                                                uideo,

Men. Tra. But I wonder how he knows my name. 70

Mess. Oh, I'll tell ye. These courtesans as soon as any strange ship arriveth at the Haven, they send a boy or a wench to inquire what they be, what their names be, whence they come, wherefore they come, etc. If they can by any means strike acquaintance with him, or allure him to their [75 houses, he is their own. We are here in a tickle place, master : 'tis best to be circumspect.

Men. Tra. I mislike not thy counsel, Messenio.

Mess. Aye, but follow it then. Soft, here comes somebody forth. Here, sirs, mariners, keep this same amongst you.   [*Giving luggage.*] [81

SCENE III

Enter EROTIUM.

Erot. Let the door stand so. Away, it shall not be shut. Make haste within there, ho ! Maids, look that all things be ready. Cover the board ; put fire under the perfuming pans : let all things be very handsome. Where is he that Cylindrus said stood without here ? [*To* Men. Tra.] Oh, [5

   qui mihi est usui et plurumum prodest.

  item hinc ultro fit, ut meret, potissumus nostrae domi

               ut sit ;

    nunc eum adibo atque ultro adloquar.

   animule mi, mihi mira uidentur   10

   te hic stare foris, fores quoi pateant,

   magi' quam domu' tua domu' quom haec tua sit

   omne paratumst, ut iussisti

    atque ut uoluisti, neque tibi

     ulla morast intus.   15

   prandium, ut iussisti, hic curatumst : ubi lubet, ire

              licet accubitum

Men. quicum haec mulier loquitur ? *Er.* equidem tecum.

           Men. quid mecum tibi

fuit umquam aut nunc est negoti ? *Er.* quia pol te unum

             ex omnibus

Venu' me uoluit magnuficare neque id haud inmerito tuo.

nam ecastor solus benefactis tuis me florentem facis. 20

Men. certo haec mulier aut insana aut ebria est, Messenio,

quae hominem ignotum compellet me tam familiariter.

Mes. dixin ego istaec heic solere fieri ? folia nunc cadunt,

praeut si tríduom hoc hic erimus : tum arbores in te cadent.

nam ita sunt hic meretrices : omnes elecebrae argentariae. 25

sed sine me dum hanc compellare. heus mulier, tibi dico.

            Er. quid est ?

Mes. ubi tu húnc hominem nouisti ? *Er.* ibidem ubi hic me

              iam diu,

what mean you, sweetheart, that ye come not in? I trust you think yourself more welcome to this house than to your own, and great reason why you should do so. Your dinner and all things are ready as you willed. Will ye go sit down?

Men. Tra. Whom doth this woman speak to? 10

Erot. Even to you, sir. To whom else should I speak?

Men. Tra. Gentlewoman, ye are a stranger to me, and I marvel at your speeches.

Erot. Yea, sir, but such a stranger as I acknowledge ye for my best and dearest friend; and well you have deserved it. 16

Men. Tra. Surely, Messenio, this woman is also mad or drunk, that useth all this kindness to me upon so small acquaintance. 19

Mess. Tush, did not I tell ye right? these be but leaves that fall upon you now, in comparison of the trees that will tumble on your neck shortly. I told ye, here were silver-tongued hacksters. But let me talk with her a little. Gentlewoman, what acquaintance have you with this man? where have you seen him? 25

Erot. Where he saw me, here in Epidamnum.

in Epidamno. *Mes.* in Epidamno ? qui huc in hanc urbem
                                                        pedem
nisi hodie numquam intro tetulit ? *Er.* heia ! delicias facis.
mi Menaechme, quin, amabo, is intro ? hic tibi erit rectius. 30
Men. haec quidem edepol recte appellat meo me mulier
                                                        nomine.
nimi' miror quid hoc sít negoti. *Mes.* óboluit marsuppium
huic istuc quod habes. *Men.* atque edepol tu me monuisti
                                                        probe.
accipedum hoc. iam scibo utrum haec me mage amet an
                                                        marsuppium.
Er. eamus intro, ut prandeamus. *Men.* bene uocas : tam [35
                                                        gratiast.
Er. qur igitur me tibi iussisti coquere dudum prandium ?
Men. egon te iussi coquere ? *Er.* certo, tíbi et párasito
                                                        tuo.
Men. quoi, malum, parasito ? certo haec mulier non sanast
                                                        satis.
Er. Peniculo. *Men.* quis iste ést Peniculus ? qui exter-
                                                gentur baxeae ?
Er. scilicet qui dudum tecum uenit, quom pallam mihi   40
detulisti quám ab uxore tua surrupuisti. *Men.* quid est ?
tibi pallam dedi quam uxori meae surrupui ? sanan es ?
certe haec mulier cantherino ritu | astans somniat.
Er. qui lubet ludibrio habere me atque ire infitias mihi
facta quae sunt ? *Men.* dic quid est id quod negem quod [45
                                                        fecerim ?

Mess. In Epidamnum ? who never till this day set his foot within the town ?

Erot. Go, go, flouting Jack. Menechmus, what need all this ? I pray, go in.   30

Men. Tra. She also calls me by my name.

Mess. She smells your purse.

Men. Tra. Messenio, come hither : here, take my purse. I'll know whether she aim at me or my purse, ere I go.

Erot. Will ye go in to dinner, sir ?   35

Men. Tra. A good motion ; yea, and thanks with all my heart.

Erot. Never thank me for that which you commanded to be provided for yourself.

Men. Tra. That I commanded ?   40

Erot. Yea, for you and your Parasite.

Men. Tra. My Parasite ?

Erot. Peniculus, who came with you this morning, when you brought me the cloak which you got from your wife.

Men. Tra. A cloak that I brought you, which I got from my wife ?   46

Erot. Tush, what needeth all this jesting ? Pray, leave off.

Er. pallam te hodie mihi dedisse uxoris.   *Men.* etiam nunc
nego.

egoquidem neque umquam uxorem hábui neque habeo neque
huc

umquam, postquam natus sum, intra portam penetraui pedem.

prandi in naui, inde huc sum egressus, te conueni.   *Er.*
éccere,

perii misera! quam tu mihi nunc nauem narras!   *Men.* [50
ligneam,

saepe tritam, saepe fixam, saepe excussam malleo;

quasi supellex pellionis, palus palo proxumust.

Er. † iam, amabo, desine † ludos facere atque i hac mecum
semul.

Men. nescio quem, mulier, alium hóminem, non me quaeritas.

Er. non ego te noui Menaechmum, Moscho prognatum [55
patre,

qui Syracusis perhibere natus esse in Sicilia,

ubi rex Agathocles regnator fuit et iterum Phintia,

tertium Liparo, qui in morte regnum Hieroni tradidit,

nunc Hiero est?   *Men.* hau falsa, mulier, praedicas.   *Mes.* pro
Iuppiter!

núm istaec mulier illinc uenit quae te nouit tam cate?   60

Men. hercle opinor, pernegari non potest.   *Mes.* ne feceris.

periisti, si intrassis intra limen.   *Men.* quin tu tace modo.

bene res geritur. adsentabor quidquid dicet mulieri,

si possum hospitium nancisci. iam dudum, mulier, tibi

non inprudens aduorsabar: hunc metuebam ni meae   65

Men. Tra. Jest or earnest, this I tell ye for a truth.   I never had wife, neither have I ; nor never was in this place till this instant ; for only thus far am I come, since I brake my fast in the ship.   52

Erot. What ship do ye tell me of ?

*Mess. Marry, I'll tell ye : an old rotten, weather-beaten ship, that we have sailed up and down in these six years. Is't not time to be going homewards think ye ?   56

Erot. Come, come, Menechmus, I pray leave this sporting and go in.

Men. Tra. Well, Gentlewoman, the truth is, you mistake my person : it is some other you look for.   60

Erot. Why, think ye I know ye not to be Menechmus, the son of Moschus, and have heard ye say, ye were born at Syracusis, where Agathocles did reign ; then Pythia, then Liparo, and now Hiero.

Men. Tra. All this is true.   65

Mess. Either she is a witch, or else she hath dwelt there and knew ye there.

Men. Tra. [*aside to* Mess.] I'll go in with her, Messenio ; I'll see further of this matter.

Mess. [*to* Men. Tra.] Ye are cast away then.   70

Men. Tra. [*aside to* Mess.] Why so ? I warrant thee, I can lose nothing ; something I shall gain ; perhaps a good lodging during my abode here.   I'll dissemble with her another while. [*To* Erotium.]   Now when you please let us go in.

uxori renuntiaret de palla et de prandio.

nunc, quando uis, eamus intro.   *Er.* étiam parasitum manes?

Men. neque ego illum maneo neque flocci facio neque, si

uenerit,

eum uolo intromitti.   *Er.* ecastor haud inuita fecero.

sed scin quid te amabo ut facias?   *Men.* impera quid uis [70

modo.

Er. pallam illam quam dudum dederas, ad phrygionem ut

deferas,

ut reconcinnetur atque ut opera addantur quae uolo.

Men. hercle qui tu recte dicis : eadem | ignorabitur,

ne uxor cognoscat te habere, si in uia conspexerit.

Er. ergo mox auferto tecum, quando abibis.   *Men.* maxume.

[75

Er. eamus intro.   *Men.* iam sequar te.   húnc uolo etiam

conloqui.

eho Messenio, | accede huc.   *Mes.* quid negoti est?   † sus-

scirit.

Men. quid eo opust?   *Mes.* opus est—*Men.* scio ut ne dicas.

Mes. tanto nequior.

Men. habeo praedam : tantum incepi óperis.   i quantum

potes,

abduc istos in tabernam actutum deuorsoriam.   80

tum facito ante solem occasum ut uenias aduorsum mihi.

Men. non tu istas meretrices nouisti, ere.   *Men.* tace, in-

quam*

mihi dolebit, non tibi, si quid ego stulte fecero.

I made strange with you, because of this fellow here, lest he should tell my wife of the cloak which I gave you.   76

Erot. Will ye stay any longer for your Peniculus, your Parasite?

Men. Tra. Not I, I'll neither stay for him, nor have him let come in, if he do come.   80

Erot. All the better. But, sir, will ye do one thing for me?

Men. Tra. What is that?

Erot. To bear that cloak which you gave me to the dyers, to have it new trimmed and altered.   85

Men. Tra. Yea, that will be well; so my wife shall not know it. Let me have it with me after dinner. I will but speak a word or two with this fellow, then I'll follow ye in. [*Exit* Erotium.] Ho, Messenio, come aside. Go and provide for thyself and these ship boys in some inn; then look that after dinner you come hither for me. 91

Mess. Ah, master, will ye be conycatched thus wilfully?

Men. Tra. Peace, foolish knave, seest thou not what a sot she is; I shall cozen her, I warrant thee

mulier haec stulta atque inscita est; quantum perspexi modo,
est hic praeda nobis. *Mes.* perii! iamne abis? periit [85
                                                        probe:
ducit lembum dierectum nauis praedatoria.
sed ego inscitus qui domino me postulem moderarier :
dicto me emit audientem, haud imperatorem sibi.
sequimini, ut, quod imperatum est, ueniam aduorsum tem-
                                                        peri.——

ACTVS III

Scaena I

Peniculvs.

Pe. Plus triginta | annis natus sum, quom | interea loci
numquam quicquam facinus feci peius neque scelestius
quám hodie, quom [in] contionem mediam me immersi miser.
ubi ego dúm hieto, Menaechmus se supterduxit mihi
atque abît ad amicam, credo, neque me uoluit ducere.   5
qui illum di omnes perduint quei primus ⟨hoc⟩ commentus est,
contionem habere, qui homines occupatos occupat!
non ad eam rem | otiosos homines decuit deligi,
qui nisi adsint quom citentur, census capiat ilico?

    * quam senatus *   * contionem *   10
                 *   *

adfatim est hominum in dies qui singulas escas edint,
quibu' negoti nihil est, qui essum neque uocantur neque
                                                        uocant :

Mess. Ay, master.   95
Men. Tra. Wilt thou be gone?   [*Exit.*]
Mess. See, see, she hath him safe enough now. Thus
he hath escaped a hundreth pirates' hands at sea; and
now one land-rover hath boarded him at first encounter.
Come away, fellows.   [*Exeunt.*] 100

ACT III

Scene I

Enter Peniculus.

Pen. Thirty years, I think, and more, have I played the
knave, yet never played I the foolish knave as I have done
this morning. I follow Menechmus, and he goes to the Hall
where now the Sessions are holden; there thrusting ourselves
into the press of people, when I was in midst of all the [5
throng, he gave me the slip, that I could never more set eye
on him, and I dare swear, came directly to dinner. That I
would he that first devised these Sessions were hanged, and
all that ever came of him, 'tis such a hindrance to men that
have belly businesses in hand. If a man be not there at [10
his call, they amerce him with a vengeance. Men that have
nothing else to do, that do neither bid any man, nor are
themselves bidden to dinner, such should come to Sessions,
                                                        E

eos oportet contioni dare operam atque comitieis.
sí id ita esset, non ego hodie perdidissem prandium,   15
quoi tam credo datum uoluísse quam me uideo uiuere.
ibo : etiamnum reliquiarum spes animum oblectat meum.
sed quid ego uideo?   Menaechmus cum corona exit foras.
sublatum est conuiuium, edepol uenio aduorsum temperi.
opseruabo quid agat hominem.   post adibo atque adloquar. 20

Scaena II
Menaechmvs II.   Peniculvs.

Men. Potine ut quiescas? ego tibi hanc hodie probe
lepideque concinnatam referam temperi.
non faxo eam esse dices : ita ignorabitur.
Pe. pallam ad phrygionem fert confecto prandio
uinoque expoto, parasito excluso foras.   5
non hercle is sum qui sum, ni | hanc iniuriam
meque ultus pulchre fuero.   opserua quid dabo.
Men. pro di inmortales ! quoí homini umquam uno die
boni dedistis plus qui minu' sperauerit ?
prandi, potaui, scortum accubui, ápstuli   10
hanc, quoiius heres numquam erit post hunc diem.
Pe. nequeo quae loquitur exaudire clanculum ;
satur nunc loquitur de me et de parti mea ?
Men. ait hanc dedisse me sibi atque eam meae
uxori surrupuisse.   quoniam sentio   15
errare, extemplo, quasi res cum ea esset mihi,

not we that have these matters to look to. If it were so, I
had not thus lost my dinner this day; which I think in [15
my conscience he did even purposely cozen me of. Yet I
mean to go see. If I can but light upon the reversion, I may
perhaps get my penny-worths. But how now? Is this
Menechmus coming away from thence? Dinner done, and
all despatched? What execrable luck have I!   20

Scene II

Enter Menechmus *the Traveller.*

Men. Tra. [*to* Erotium *within*] Tush, I warrant ye, it
shall be done as ye would wish. I'll have it so altered and
trimmed anew, that it shall by no means be known again.

Pen. [*aside*] He carries the cloak to the dyers, dinner
done, the wine drunk up, the Parasite shut out of doors. [5
Well, let me live no longer, but I'll revenge this injurious
mockery. But first I'll hearken awhile what he saith.

Men. Tra. Good gods, who ever had such luck as I!
Such cheer, such a dinner, such kind entertainment! And
for a farewell, this cloak which I mean shall go with me. 10

Pen. [*aside*] He speaks so softly, I cannot hear what he
saith. I am sure he is now flouting at me for the loss of my
dinner.

Men. Tra. She tells me how I gave it her, and stole it
from my wife. When I perceived she was in an error [15

E 2

coepi adsentari : mulier quidquid dixerat,
idem ego dicebam. quid multis uerbis ⟨opust⟩ ?
minore nusquam bene fui dispendio.
Pe. adibo ad hominem, nam turbare gestio.   20
Men. quis hic est qui aduorsus it mihi ? *Pe.* quid ais, homo
leuior quam pluma, pessume et nequissume,
flagitium hominis, subdole ac minimi preti ?
quid de te merui qua me caussa perderes ?
ut surrupuisti te mihi dudum de foro !   25
fecisti funus med apsenti prandio.
qur ausu's facere, quoii ego aeque heres eram ?
Men. adulescens, quaeso, quid tibi mecum est rei
qui mihi male dicas homini ignoto | insciens ?
an tibi malam rem uis pro male dictis dari ?   30
Pe. post eam quam edepol te dedisse intellego.
Men. responde, adulescens, quaeso, quid nomen tibist ?
Pe. etiam derides quasi nomen non gnoueris ?
Men. non edepol ego te quod sciam umquam ante hunc diem
uidi neque gnoui ; uerum certo, quisquis es,   35
si aequom facias, mihi odiosus ne sies.
Pe. Menaechme, uigila. *Men.* uigilo hercle equidem quod
                                 sciam.
Pe. non me nouisti ? *Men.* non negem si nouerim.
Pe. tuom parasitum non nouisti ? *Men.* non tibi
sanum est, adulescens, sinciput, intellego.   40
Pe. responde, surrupuistin uxori tuae
pallam istanc hodie | ac dedisti Erotio ?

tho' I knew not how, I began to soothe her, and to say every- thing as she said. Meanwhile, I fared well, and that o' free cost.

Pen. Well, I'll go talk with him.   [*Coming forward.*]

Men. Tra. Who is this same that comes to me?   20

Pen. Oh, well met, fickle-brain, false and treacherou dealer, crafty and unjust promise-breaker. How have I deserved, you should so give me the slip, come before, and despatch the dinner, deal so badly with him that hath reverenced ye like a son?   25

Men. Tra. Good fellow, what meanest thou by these speeches? Rail not on me, unless thou intend'st to receive a railer's hire.

Pen. I have received the injury, sure I am, already.

Men. Tra. Prithee tell me, what is thy name?   30

Pen. Well, well, mock on, sir, mock on: do ye not know my name?

Men. Tra. In troth I never saw thee in all my life; much less do I know thee.

Pen. Fie! awake, Menechmus, awake; ye oversleep yourself!   36

Men. Tra. I am awake: I know what I say.

Pen. Know you not Peniculus?

Men. Tra. Peniculus, or Pediculus, I know thee not.

Pen. Did ye filch a cloak from your wife this morning, and bring it hither to Erotium?   41

Men. neque hercle ego uxorem habeo neque ego Erotio
dedi nec pallam surrupui. *Pe.* satin sanus es ?
occisast haec res. non ego te indutum foras   45
exeire uidi pallam ? *Men.* uae capiti tuo !
omnis cinaedos esse censes quia tu és ?
tun med indutum fuisse pallam praedicas ?
Pe. ego hercle uero. *Men.* non tu abis quo dignus es ?
aut te piari iúbe, homo ínsanissume.   50
Pe. numquam edepol quisquam me exorabit quin tuae
uxori rem omnem iám, uti sit gesta, eloquar ;
omnes in té istaec recident contumeliae :
faxo haud inultus prandium comederis.——
Men. quid hoc ést negoti ? satine, uti quemque conspicor, 55
ita me ludificant ? sed concrepuit ostium.

Scaena III

Ancilla.   Menaechmvs II.

An. Menaechme, amare ait te multum Erotium,
†ut hoc una opera ad auruficem deferas, †
atque huc ut addas auri pondo | unciam
iubeasque spinter nouom reconcinnarier.
Men. et istúc et aliud si quid curari uolet
me curaturum dicito, quidquid uolet.   5
An. scin quid hoc sit spinter ? *Men.* nescic nisi aureum.
An. hoc est quod olim clanculum ex armario
te surrupuisse aiebas uxori tuae.

Men. Tra. Neither have I wife, neither gave I my cloak to Erotium, neither filched I any from anybody.

Pen. Will ye deny that which you did in my company?

Men. Tra. Wilt thou say I have done this in thy company? 45

Pen. Will I say it? yea, I will stand to it.

Men. Tra. Away, filthy mad drivel, away; I will talk no longer with thee.

Pen. Not a world of men shall stay me, but I'll go tell his wife of all the whole matter, sith he is at this point [50 with me. I will make this same as unblest a dinner as ever he eat.   [*Exit.*]

Men. Tra. It makes me wonder, to see how everyone that meets me cavils thus with me. Wherefore comes forth the maid now?   55

Scene III

Enter Ancilla, Erotium's *maid.*

Anc. Menechmus, my mistress commends her heartily to you, and seeing you go that way to the dyer's, she also desireth you to take this chain with you, and put it to mending at the goldsmith's; she would have two or three ounces of gold more in it, and the fashion amended.   5

Men. Tra. Either this or anything else within my power, tell her, I am ready to accomplish.

Anc. Do ye know this chain, sir?

Men. Tra. Yea, I know it to be gold.

Anc. This is the same you once took out of your wife's casket.   11

Men. numquam hercle factum est. *An.* non meministi, [10
opsecro?
redde igitur spinter, si non meministi. *Men.* mane.
immo equidem memini. nempe hoc est quod illí dedei.
istuc : ubi illae ármillae sunt quas una dedei ?
An. numquam dedisti. *Men.* nam pol hoc unum dedei.
An. dicam curare? *Men.* dicito : curabitur. 15
et palla et spinter faxo referantur simul.
An. amabo, mi Menaechme, inauris da mihi
faciendas pondo duom nummum, stalagmia,
ut te lubenter uideam, quom ad nos ueneris.
Men. fiat. cedo aurum ; ego manupretium dabo. 20
An. da sodes aps te ; poste reddidero tibi.
Men. immo cedo aps te : ego post tibi reddam duplex.
An. non habeo. *Men.* át tu, quando habebis, tum dato.
An. numquid [me] uis ?—*Men.* haec me curaturum dicito—
ut quantum possint quique liceant ueneant. 25
iamne introabiit ? abiit, operuit fores.
di me quidem omnes adiuuant, augent, amant.
sed quid ego cesso, dum datur mi occasio
tempusque, abire ab his locis lenonieis ?
propera, Menaechme, fer pedem, confer gradum. 30
demam hanc coronam atque abiciam ad laeuam manum,
ut, si [quis] sequantur me, hac abiisse censeant.
ibo et conueniam seruom si potero meum,
ut haec, quae bona dant di mihi, | ex me sciat.—

Men. Tra. Who, did I?

Anc. Have you forgotten?

Men. Tra. I never did it.

Anc. Give it me again then.   15

Men. Tra. Tarry : yes, I remember it ; 'tis it I gave your mistress.

Anc. Oh, are you advised?

Men. Tra. Where are the bracelets that I gave her like-wise?   20

Anc. I never knew of any.

Men. Tra. Faith, when I gave this, I gave them too.

Anc. Well, sir, I'll tell her this shall be done?

Men. Tra. Ay, ay, tell her so ; she shall have the cloak and this both together.   25

Anc. I pray, Menechmus, put a little jewel for my ear to making for me : ye know I am always ready to pleasure you.

Men. Tra. I will, give me the gold; I'll pay for the workmanship.

Anc. Lay out for me ; I'll pay it ye again.   30

Men. Tra. Alas, I have none now.

Anc. When you have, will ye?

Men. Tra. I will.   Go bid your mistress make no doubt of these.   I warrant her, I'll make the best hand I can of them.   [*Exit* Ancilla.]   Is she gone?   Do not all the [35 gods conspire to load me with good luck? well I see 'tis high time to get me out of these coasts, lest all these matters should be lewd devices to draw me into some snare.   There shall my garland lie, because if they seek me, they may think I am gone that way.   *I will now go see if I can find my man Messenio, that I may tell him how I have sped.   41

ACTVS IV

Scaena I

Matrona. Peniculus

Ma. Egone hic me patiar frustra in matrimoni
ubi uir compilet clanculum quidquid domist
atque ea ad amicam deferat ? *Pe.* quin tu taces ?
manufesto faxo iam opprimes : sequere hac modo.
pallam ad phrygionem cum corona | ebrius   5
ferebat hodie tibi quam surrupuit domo.
sed eccám coronam quám habuit.   num mentior ?
em hac abiit, si uis persequi uestigiis.
atque edepol eccum óptume reuortitur ;
sed pallam non fert. *Ma.* quid ego nunc cum illoc agam ? 10
Pe. idem quod semper : male habeas ; sic censeo.
huc concedamus : ex insidieis aucupa.

Scaena II

Menaechmvs I. Peniculvs. Matrona.

Men. Vt hoc utimur maxume more moro,
molesto atque multo atque uti quique sunt op-
-tumi maxume morem habent hunc !
clientes sibi omnes uolunt esse multos :

ACT IV

Scene I

Enter Mulier, *the Wife of* Menechmus *the Citizen, and*
Peniculus.

Mul. Thinks he I will be made such a sot, and to be still
his drudge, while he prowls and purloins all that I have, to
give his trulls?

Pen. Nay, hold your peace, we'll catch him in the nick.
This way he came, in his garland forsooth, bearing the [5
cloak to the dyers. And see, I pray, where the garland lies;
this way he is gone. See, see, where he comes again now
without the cloak.

Mul. What shall I now do?

Pen. What? That which ye ever do; bait him for life. 10

Mul. Surely I think it best so.

Pen. Stay, we will stand aside a little; ye shall catch him
unawares.

Scene II

Enter Menechmus *the Citizen.*

Men. Cit. It would make a man at his wit's end, to see
how brabbling causes are handled yonder at the Court. If
a poor man never so honest have a matter come to be scanned,

59

bonine an mali sint, id hau quaeritant ; res   5
magis quaeritur quam clientum fides
    quoius modi clueat.
  si ést pauper atque hau malus nequam habetur,
  sin diues malust, is cliens frugi habetur.
qui nec leges neque aequom bonum usquam colunt,   10
    sollicitos patronos habent.
datum denegant quod datum est, litium pleni, rapaces
    uiri, fraudulenti,
qui aut faenore aut peiiuriis habent rem paratam,
      mens est in quo   *   15
  eis ubi dicitur dies, simul patronis dicitur,
    quippe qui pro illis loquimur quae male fecerunt :
    aut ad populum aut in iure aut ad iudicem rest.
sicut me hodie nimi' sollicitum cliens quidam habuit neque
              quod uolui
  agere aut quicum licitumst, ita med attinit, ita detinit.   20
apud aedilis pro eius factis plurumisque pessumisque
deixei caussam, condiciones tetuli tortas, confragosas :
aut plus aut minu' quam opus erat dícto dixeram cóntrouor-
             siam, ut
    sponsio fieret.   quid ill' qui praedem dedit ?
nec magis manufestum ego hominem úmquam ullum teneri [25
              uidi :
omnibus male factis testes tres aderant acerrumi.
    di illum omnes perdant, ita mihi
    hunc hodie corrumpit diem,

there is he outfaced and overlaid with countenance : if a rich

man never so vile a wretch come to speak, there they are [5

all ready to favour his cause.   What with facing out bad causes

for the oppressors, and patronizing some just actions for the

wronged, the lawyers they pocket up all the gains.   For mine

own part, I come not away empty, though I have been kept

long against my will : for taking in hand to despatch a [10

matter this morning for one of my acquaintance, I was no

sooner entered into it, but his adversaries laid so hard

unto his charge, and brought such matter against him, that do

what I could, I could not wind myself out till now.   I am

meque adeo, quí hodie forum
umquam oculis inspexi meis.   30
diem corrupi | optumum :
iussi apparari prandium,
amica exspectat me, scio.
ubi primum est licitum ilico
properaui abire de foro.   35
iratast, credo, nunc mihi ;
placabit palla quam dedi,
quám hodie uxori apstuli atque detuli huic Erotio.

Pe. quid ais ? *Ma.* uiro me malo male nuptam. *Pe.*
              satin audis quae illic loquitur ?
Ma. sati'. *Men.* si sapiam, hinc intro abeam, ubi mi [40
              bene sit. *Pe.* mane : male erit potius.
Ma. né illam ecastor faenerato ápstulisti. *Pe.* sic datur.
Ma. clanculum te istaec flagitia facere censebas pote ?
Men. quid illuc est, uxor, negoti ? *Ma.* men rogas ?
              Men. uin hunc rogem ?
Ma. aufer hinc palpationes. *Pe.* perge tu. *Men.* quid tu
              mihi
tristis es ? *Ma.* te scire oportet. *Pe.* scit sed dissimulat [45
              malus.
Men. quid negotist ? *Ma.* pallam—*Men.* pallam ? *Ma.*
              quidam pallam—*Pe.* quid paues ?
Men. nil equidem paueo. *Pe.* nisi unum : palla pallorem
              incutit.
at tu né clam me comesses prandium.   perge in uirum.

sore afraid Erotium thinks much unkindness in me, [15
that I stayed so long ; yet she will not be angry considering
the gift I gave her to-day.

Pen. How think ye by that ?

Mul. I think him a most vile wretch thus to abuse me.

Men. Cit. I will hie me thither.   20

Mul. Yea, go, pilferer, go with shame enough ; nobody
sees your lewd dealings and vile thievery.

Men. Cit. How now, wife, what ail ye ? what is the
matter ?

Mul. Ask ye me what's the matter ?   Fie upon thee.   25

Pen. Are ye not in a fit of an ague, your pulses beat so
sore ?   To him, I say !

Men. Cit. Pray, wife, why are ye so angry with me ?

Mul. Oh, you know not ?

Pen. He knows, but he would dissemble it.   30

Men. Cit. What is it ?

Mul. My cloak.

Men. Cit. Your cloak ?

Mul. My cloak, man ; why do ye blush ?

Pen. He cannot cloak his blushing.   Nay, I might not go
to dinner with you, do you remember ?   To him, I say.   36

Men. non taces? *Pe.* non hercle uero taceo. nutat ne
       loquar.
Men. non hercle egoquidem usquam quicquam nuto neque [50
       nicto tibi.
Ma. né ego ecastor mulier misera. *Men.* qui tu misera es?
       mi expedi.
Pe. nihil hoc confidentius : quin quae uides ea pernegat.
Men. per Iouem deosque omnis adiuro, uxor (satin hoc est
       tibi?),
me isti non nutasse. *Pe.* credit iam tibi de 'isti' : illuc redi.
Men. quó ego redeam? *Pe.* equidem ád phrygionem [55
       censeo ; et pallam refer.
Men. quaé istaec palla est? *Pe.* taceo iam, quando haec
       rem non meminit suam.
Men. numquis seruorum deliquit? num ancillae aut seruei tibi
responsant? eloquere. inpune non erit. *Ma.* nugas agis.
Men. tristis admodum est. non mihi istuc sati' placet— *Ma.*
       nugas agis.
Men. certe familiarium-aliquoi írata es. *Ma.* nugas agis. 60
Men. num mihi es irata saltem? *Ma.* nunc tu non nugas
       agis.
Men. non edepol deliqui quicquam. *Ma.* em rusum nunc
       nugas agis
Men. dic, mea uxor, quid tibi aegre est? *Pe.* bellus
       blanditur tibi.
Men. potin ut mihi molestus ne sis? num te appello?
       Ma. aufer manum

Men. Cit. Hold thy peace, Peniculus.

Pen. Ha, hold my peace! Look ye, he beckons on me to hold my peace.

Men. Cit. I neither beckon nor wink on him. 40

Mul. Out, out, what a wretched life is this that I live.

Men. Cit. Why, what ail ye, woman?

Mul. Are ye not ashamed to deny so confidently, that which is apparent?

Men. Cit. I protest unto you before all the gods—is not this enough?—that I beckoned not on him. 46

Pen. Oh, sir, this is another matter: touch him in the former cause.

Men. Cit. What former cause?

Pen. The cloak, man, the cloak: fetch the cloak again from the dyers. 51

Men. Cit. What cloak?

Mul. Nay, I'll say no more, sith ye know nothing of your own doings.

Men. Cit. Tell me, wife, hath any of your servants abused you? Let me know. 56

Mul. Tush, tush.

Men. Cit. I would not have you to be thus disquieted.

Mul. Tush, tush.

Men. Cit. You are fallen out with some of your friends.

Mul. Tush, tush. 61

Men. Cit. Sure I am, I have not offended you.

Mul. No, you have dealt very honestly.

Men. Cit. Indeed, wife, I have deserved none of these words. Tell me, are ye not well? 65

Pen. What, shall he flatter ye now?

Men. Cit. I speak not to thee, knave. Good wife, come hither.

Mul. Away, away; keep your hands off.

F

Pe. sic datur. properato apsente me comesse prandium, 65
post ante aedis cum corona me derideto ebrius.
Men. neque edepol ego prandi neque hodie huc intro tetuli
pedem.
Pe. tun negas? *Men.* nego hercle uero. *Pe.* nihil hoc
homine audacius.
non ego te modo hic ante aedis cum corona florea
uidi astare? quom negabas mihi esse sanum sinciput 70
et negabas me nouisse, peregrinum aibas esse te?
Men. quin ut dudum diuorti aps te, redeo nunc demum domum.
Pe. noui ego te. non mihi censebas esse qui te ulciscerer.
omnia hercle uxori dixi. *Men.* quid dixisti? *Pe.* nescio,
eam ipsus [i] roga. *Men.* quid hoc est, uxor? quidnam
hic narrauit tibi? [75]
quid id est? quid taces; quin dicis quid sit? *Ma.* quasi
tu nescias.
palla mihi est domo surrupta. *Men.* palla surrupta est tibi?
Ma. me rogas? *Men.* pol hau rogem te si sciam. *Pe.* o
hominem malum,
ut dissimulat! non potes celare: rem nouit probe.
omnia hercle ego edictaui. *Men.* quid id est? *Ma.* [80
quando nil pudet
neque uis tua uoluntate ipse profiteri, audi atque ades.
et quid tristis ⟨sim⟩ et quid hic mihi dixerit faxo scias.
palla mihi est domo surrupta. *Men.* palla surruptast mihi?
Pe. uiden ut ⟨te⟩ scelestus captat? huic surruptast, non tibi.
nam profecto tibi surrupta si esset—salua non foret. 85

Pen. So, bid me to dinner with you again, then slip [70 away from me; when you have done, come forth bravely in your garland, to flout me. Alas, you knew not me even now.

Men. Cit. Why, ass, I neither have yet dined, nor came I there, since we were there together. 74

Pen. Who ever heard one so impudent? Did ye not meet me here even now, and would make me believe I was mad, and said ye were a stranger, and ye knew me not?

Men. Cit. Of a truth, since we went together to the Sessions Hall, I never returned till this very instant, as you two met me.

Pen. Go to, go to, I know ye well enough. Did ye think I would not cry quittance with you? Yes, faith : I have told your wife all. 82

Men. Cit. What hast thou told her?

Pen. I cannot tell. Ask her.

Men. Cit. Tell me, wife, what hath he told ye of me? Tell me, I say; what was it? 86

Mul. As though you knew not my cloak is stolen from me !

Men. Cit. Is your cloak stolen from ye?

Mul. Do ye ask me?

Men. Cit. If I knew, I would not ask. 90

Pen. O crafty companion ! how he would shift the matter? Come, come, deny it not : I tell ye. I have bewrayed all.

Men. Cit. What hast thou bewrayed?

Mul. Seeing ye will yield to nothing, be it never so mani-fest, hear me, and ye shall know in few words both the [95 cause of my grief, and what he hath told me. I say my cloak is stolen from me.

Men. Cit. My cloak is stolen from me?

Pen. Look how he cavils ! She saith it is stolen from her.

F 2

Men. nil mihi tecum est. sed tu quid ais? *Ma.* palla,
inquam, periit domo.

Men. quis eam surrupuit? *Ma.* pol istuc ille scit qui illam
apstulit.

Men. quis is homo est? *Ma.* Menaechmus quidam. *Men.*
édepol factum nequiter.

quis is Menaechmust? *Ma.* tu istic, inquam. *Men.* egone?
Ma. tu. *Men.* quis arguit?

Ma. egomet. *Pe.* et ego. atque huic amicae detulisti [90
Erotio.

Men. egon dedi? *Ma.* tu tú istic, inquam. *Pe.* uin adferri
noctuam,

quae ' tu tu ' usque dicat tibi? nam nos iam defessi sumus.

Men. per Iouem deosque omnis adiuro, uxor (satin hoc est
tibi?),

non dedisse. *Pe.* immo hercle uero, nos non falsum dicere.

Men. sed ego illam non condonaui, sed sic utendam dedi.   95

Ma. equidem ecastor tuam nec chlamydem do foras nec
pallium

quoiquam utendum. mulierem aequom est uestimentum
muliebre

dare foras, uirum uirile. quin refers pallam domum?

Men. ego faxo referetur. *Ma.* ex re tua, ut opinor, feceris;

nam domum numquam introibis nisi feres pallam simul.   100

eo domum. *Pe.* quid mihi futurum est qui tibi hanc operam
dedi?

Ma. opera reddetur, quando quid tibi erit surruptum domo.—

Men. Cit. I have nothing to say to thee : I say, wife, tell me.   101

Mul. I tell ye, my cloak is stolen out of my house.

Men. Cit. Who stole it?

Mul. He knows best that carried it away.

Men. Cit. Who was that?   105

Mul. Menechmus.

Men. Cit. 'Twas very ill done of him. What Menechmus was that?

Mul. You.

Men. Cit. I! who will say so?   110

Mul. I will.

Pen. And I, that you gave it to Erotium.

Men. Cit. I gave it?

Mul. You.   114

Pen. You, you, you : shall we fetch a kennel of beagles that may cry nothing but you, you, you, you! For we are weary of it.

Men. Cit. Hear me one word, wife. I protest unto you by all the gods, I gave it her not : indeed I lent it her to use a while.   120

Mul. Faith, sir, I never give nor lend your apparel out of doors. Methinks ye might let me dispose of mine own garments as you do of yours. I pray then fetch it me home again.

Men. Cit. You shall have it again without fail.   125

Mul. 'Tis best for you that I have : otherwise think not to roost within these doors again.

Pen. Hark ye, what say ye to me now, for bringing these matters to your knowledge?

Pe. id quidem edepol numquam erit, nam nihil est quod
perdam domi.

cum uiro cum uxore, di uos perdant! properabo ad forum,
nam ex hac familia me plane éxcidisse intellego.—   105
Men. male mi uxor sese fecisse censet, quom exclusit foras;
quasi non habeam quo intromittar alium meliorem locum.
si tibi displiceo, patiundum: at placuero huic Erotio,
quae me non excludet ab se, sed apud se occludet domi.
nunc ibo, orabo ut mihi pallam reddat quam dudum dedi;   110
aliam illi redimam meliorem.   heus! ecquis hic est ianitor?
aperite atque Erotium aliquis euocate ante ostium.

SCAENA III

EROTIVM.   MENAECHMVS I.

Er. Quis hic me quaerit?   *Men.* sibi inimicus magi' quam
aetati tuae.

Er. mi Menaechme, qur ante aedis astas? sequere intro.
Men. mane.

scin quid est quod ego ad te uenio?   *Er.* scio, ut tibi ex me
sit uolup.

Men. immo edepol pallam illam, amabo te, quam tibi dudum
dedi,

mihi eam redde. uxor resciuit rem omnem, ut factum est,   [5
ordine.

ego tibi redimam bis tanta pluris pallam quam uoles,

Mul. I say, when thou hast anything stolen from thee, come to me, and I will help thee to seek it.   And so, [131 farewell.   [*Exit.*]

Pen. God a mercy for nothing : that can never be, for I have nothing in the world worth the stealing. So now with husband, wife, and all, I am clean out of favour.   A mischief on ye all.   [136   *Exit.*

Men. Cit. My wife thinks she is notably revenged on me, now she shuts me out of doors, as though I had not a better place to be welcome to. If she shut me out, I know who will shut me in.   Now will I entreat Erotium to let me [140 have the cloak again to stop my wife's mouth withal ; and then will I provide a better for her.   Ho ! who is within there ? Somebody tell Erotium I must speak with her.

Scene III

Enter Erotium.

Erot. Who calls ?

Men. Cit. Your friend more than his own.

Erot. O Menechmus, why stand ye here ? pray come in.

Men. Cit. Tarry, I must speak with ye here.

Erot. Say your mind.   5

Men. Cit. Wot ye what ? my wife knows all the matter now, and my coming is, to request you that I may have again the cloak which I brought you, that so I may appease her : and I promise you, I'll give ye another worth two of it.

Er. tibi dedi equidem illam, ad phrygionem út ferres, paullo
prius,

et illud spinter, ut ad auruficem ferres, ut fieret nouom.

Men. mihi tu ut dederis pallam et spinter ? numquam factum
reperies.

nam ego quidem postquam illam dudum tibi dedi, atque [10
abii ad forum :

nunc redeo, nunc te postillac uideo. *Er.* uideo quam rem agis.

quia commisi, ut me defrudes, ad eam rem adfectas uiam.

Men. neque edepol te defrudandi caussa posco (quin tibi

dico uxorem resciuisse) — *Er.* nec te ultro oraui ut dares :

tute ultro ad me detulisti, dedisti eam dono mihi ;   15

eandem nunc reposcis : patiar. tibi habe, aúfer, utere

uel tu uel tua uxor, uel etiam in loculos compingite.

tu huc post hunc diem pedem intro non feres, ne frustra sis ;

quando tu me bene merentem tibi habes despicatui,

nisi feres argentum, frustra me ductare non potes.   20

aliam posthac inuenito quám habeas frustratui.—

Men. nimis iracunde hercle tandem. heús tu, tibi dico, mane,

redi. etiamne astas ? etiam audes mea reuorti gratia ?

abiit intro, occlusit aedis. nunc ego sum exclusissumus :

neque domi neque apud amicam mihi iam quicquam creditur. 25

ibo et consulam hanc rem amicos quid faciendum censeant.—

Erot. Why, I gave it you to carry to your dyers; and my chain likewise, to have it altered.   11

Men. Cit. Gave me the cloak and your chain?   In truth I never saw ye since I left it here with you, and so went to the Sessions, from whence I am but now returned.   14

Erot. Ah then, sir, I see you wrought a device to defraud me of them both.   Did I therefore put ye in trust?   Well, well.

Men. Cit. To defraud ye?   No: but I say, my wife hath intelligence of the matter.   19

Erot. Why, sir, I asked them not; ye brought them of your own free motion.   Now ye require them again, take them, make sops of them, you and your wife together. Think ye I esteem them or you either?   Go; come to me again when I send for you.

Men. Cit. What! so angry with me, sweet Erotium? Stay, I pray stay.   26

* *Erot.* Stay?   Faith, sir, no: think ye I will stay at your request?

Men. Cit. What, gone in chafing, and clapped to the doors? now I am every way shut out for a very bench-whistler: neither shall I have entertainment here nor at home. I were best go try some other friends, and ask counsel what to do.   33

ACTVS V

Scaena I

MENAECHMVS II.   MATRONA.

Men. Nimi' stulte dudum feci quom marsupium
Messenioni cum argento concredidi.
immersit aliquo sese, credo, in ganeum.
Ma. prouisam quam mox uir meus redeat domum.
sed eccum uideo.   salua sum, pallam refert.   5
Men. demiror ubi nunc ambulet Messenio.
Ma. adibo atque hominem accipiam quibu' dictis meret.
non te pudet prodire in conspectum meum,
flagitium hominis, cum istoc ornatu?   *Men.* quid est?
quae te res agitat, mulier?   *Ma.* etiamne, inpudens,   10
muttire uerbum unum audes aut mecum loqui?
Men. quid tandem admisi in me ut loqui non audeam?
Ma. rogas me?   hóminis inpudentem audaciam!
Men. non tu scis, mulier, Hecubam quapropter canem
Graii esse praedicabant?   *Ma.* non equidem scio.   15
Mén. quia idem faciebat Hecuba quod tu nunc facis:
omnia mala ingerebat quemquem aspexerat.
itaque adeo iure coepta appellari est Canes.
Ma. non ego istaec flagitia possum perpeti.
nam med aetatem uiduam | esse mauelim   20

74

ACT V
Scene I
Enter Menechmus *the Traveller,* Mulier.

Men. Tra. Most foolishly was I overseen in giving my purse and money to Messenio, whom I can nowhere find. I fear he is fallen into some lewd company.

Mul. I marvel that my husband comes not yet; but see where he is now, and brings my cloak with him.   5

Men. Tra. I muse where the knave should be.

Mul. I will go ring a peal through both his ears for this dishonest behaviour. Oh, sir, ye are welcome home with your thievery on your shoulders. Are ye not ashamed to let all the world see and speak of your lewdness?   10

Men. Tra. How now? what lacks this woman?

Mul. Impudent beast, stand ye to question about it? For shame hold thy peace.

Men. Tra. What offence have I done, woman, that I should not speak to you?   15

Mul. Askest thou what offence? O shameless boldness!

Men. Tra. Good woman, did ye never hear why the Grecians termed Hecuba to be a bitch?

Mul. Never.   19

Men. Tra. Because she did as you do now; on whomsoever she met withall, she railed, and therefore well deserved that dogged name.

Mul. These foul abuses and contumelies I can never endure; nay, rather will I live a widow's life to my dying day.   24

Men. Tra. What care I whether thou livest as a widow, or as a wife? This passeth, that I meet with none, but thus they vex me with strange speeches.

Mul. What strange speeches? I say I will surely live a widow's life, rather than suffer thy vile dealings.

quam istaec flagitia tua pati quae tu facis.

Men. quid id ad me, tu te nuptam possis perpeti

an sis abitura a tuo uiro? an mos hic ita est

peregrino ut aduenienti narrent fabulas?

Ma. quas fabulas?   non, inquam, patiar praeterhac,   25

quin uidua uiuam quam tuos móres perferam.

Men. mea quidem hercle caussa uidua uiuito

uel usque dum regnum optinebit Iuppiter.

Ma. at mihi negabas dudum surrupuisse te,

nunc eandem ante oculos adtines : non te pudet?   30

Men. eu hercle! mulier, multum et audax et mala's.

tun tibi hanc surruptam dicere audes quam mihi

dedit alia mulier ut concinnandam darem?

Ma. ne istuc mecastor—iam patrem accersam meum

atque ei narrabo tua flagitia quae facis.   35

i, Decio, quaere meum patrem, tecum simul

ut ueniat ad me : íta rem | esse dicito.

iam ego aperiam istaec tua flagitia.   *Men.* sanan es?

quae mea flagitia?   *Ma.* pallam | atque aurum meum

domo suppilas tuae uxóri | et tuae   40

degeris amicae.   satin haec recte fabulor?

Men. quaeso hercle, mulier, si scis, monstra quod bibam

tuam qui possim perpeti petulantiam.

quem tú hominem (med) arbitrere nescio;

ego te simitu noui cum Porthaone.   45

Ma. si me derides, at pol illum non potes,

patrem meum qui huc aduenit.   quin respicis?

Men. Tra. Prithee for my part, live a widow till the world's end, if thou wilt.   31

Mul. Even now thou denied'st that thou stolest it from me, and now thou bringest it home openly in my sight.   Art not ashamed?   34

Men. Tra. Woman, you are greatly to blame to charge me with stealing of this cloak, which this day another gave me to carry to be trimmed.

Mul. Well, I will first complain to my father.   Ho, boy, who is within there?   Decio, go run quickly to my father; desire him of all love to come over quickly to my [40 house.   I'll tell him first of your pranks; I hope he will not see me thus handled.

Men. Tra. What a God's name meaneth this mad woman thus to vex me?   44

Mul. I am mad because I tell ye of your vile actions and lewd pilfering away my apparel and my jewels, to carry to your filthy drabs.

Men. Tra. For whom this woman taketh me I know not.   I know her as much as I know Hercules' wife's father.   50

Mul. Do ye not know me?   That's well.   I hope ye know my father: here he comes.   Look, do ye know him?

nouistin tu illum? *Men.* noui cum Calcha simul :
eodem die illum uidi quo te ante hunc diem.
Ma. negas nouisse me ? negas patrem meum ?   50
Men. idem hercle dicam sí auom uis adducere.
Ma. ecastor pariter hoc atque alias res soles.

Scaena II

Senex.   Matrona.   Menaechmvs II.

Se. Vt aetas mea est atque ut hoc usu' facto est
gradum proferam, progrediri properabo.
sed id quam mihi facile sit hau sum falsus.
nam pernicitas deserit : consitus sum
senectute, onustum gero corpu', uires   5
reliquere : ut aetas mala est ! mers mala ergost.
nam res plurumas pessumas, quom aduenit, ad-
-fert, quas si autumem omnis, nimis longu' sermost.
sed haec res mihi in pectore et corde curaest,
    quidnam hoc sit negoti quod sic filia   10
    repente expetit mé, ut ad sese irem.
    nec quid id sit mihi certius facit, quid
        uelit.   quid me accersit ?
uerum propemodum iam scio quid siet rei.
credo cum uiro litigium natum esse aliquod.   15
ita istaec solent, quae uiros supseruire
sibi postulant, dote fretae, feroces

Men. Tra. As much as I knew Calchas of Troy.   Even him and thee I know both alike.   55

Mul. Dost know neither of us both, me nor my father?

Men. Tra. Faith, nor thy grandfather neither.

Mul. This is like the rest of your behaviour.

Scene II

Enter Senex. — ~~Futha~~ of Mulier

* *Sen.* Though, bearing so great a burthen as old age, I can make no great haste, yet as I can, I will go to my daughter, who I know hath some earnest business with me, that she sends in such haste, not telling the cause why I should come. But I durst lay a wager, I can guess near the matter: I [5 suppose it is some brabble between her husband and her. These young women that bring great dowries to their husbands, are so masterful and obstinate, that they will have their own wills in everything, and make men servants to their

et illi quoque haud apstinent saepe culpa.

    uerum est modu' tamen, quoad pati uxorem oportet;

      nec pol filia umquam patrem accersit ad se   20

         nisi aut quid commissí aut iurgi est caussa.

    sed id quidquid est iam sciam.   atque eccam eampse

ante aedis et eius tristem uirum uideo. id est quod suspicabar.

appellabo hanc. *Ma.* ibo aduorsum. salue multum, mi

                                     pater.

Se. salua sis. saluen aduenio? saluen accersi iubes?   25

quid tu tristis es? quid ille autem aps te iratus destitit?

nescioquid uos uelitati éstis inter uos duos.

loquere, uter meruistis culpam, paucis, non longos logos.

Ma. nusquam equidem quicquam deliqui: hoc primum te

                             apsoluo, pater.

uerum uiuere hic non possum neque durare ullo modo.   30

proin tu me hinc abducas. *Se.* quid istuc autem est? *Ma.*

                             ludibrio, pater,

habeor. *Se.* unde? *Ma.* ab illo quoi me mandauisti, meo uiro.

Se. ecce autem litigium! quotiens tandem | edixi tibi

ut caueres neuter ad me iretis cum querimonia?   34

Ma. quí ego istuc, mi pater, cauere possum? *Se.* men

                            interrogas?

Ma. nisi non uis. *Se.* quotiens monstraui tibi uiro ut morem

                               geras,

quid ille faciat né id opserues, quó eat, quid rerum gerat.

Ma. at enim ille hinc amat meretricem ex proxumo.

                         Se. sane sapit

weak affections : and young men too, I must needs say, [10
be naught nowadays.   Well, I'll go see, but yonder methinks
stands my daughter, and her husband too.   Oh, 'tis even as I
guessed.

Mul. Father, ye are welcome.

Sen. How now, daughter ?   What ? is all well ; why [15
is your husband so sad ? have ye bin chiding ? tell me, which
of you is in fault ?

Mul. First, father, know, that I have not any way mis-
behaved myself; but the truth is, that I can by no means
endure this bad man to die for it ; and therefore desire [20
you to take me home to you again.

Sen. What is the matter ?

Mul. He makes me a stale and a laughing-stock to all the
world.

Sen. Who doth ?   25

Mul. This good husband here, to whom you married me.

Sen. See, see ; how oft have I warned you of falling out
with your husband ?

Mul. I cannot avoid it, if he doth so foully abuse me. 29

Sen. I always told ye, ye must bear with him, ye must let
him alone ; ye must not watch him, nor dog him, nor meddle
with his courses in any sort.

Mul. He haunts naughty harlots under my nose.

G

atque ob istánc industriam etiam faxo amabit amplius.

Ma. atque ibi potat.   *Se.* tua quidem ille caussa potabit   [40
                                               minus,

si illic siue alibi lubebit ? quaé haec, malum, impudentiast ?

una opera prohibere ad cenam ne promittat postules

neu quemquam accipiat alienum apud se.   seruirin tibi

postulas uiros ? dare una ópera pensum postules,

inter ancillas sedere iubeas, lanam carere.   45

Ma. non equidem mihi te aduocatum, pater, adduxi, sed uiro.

hinc stas, illim caussam dicis.   *Se.* si ille quid deliquerit,

multo tanta illum accusabo quam te accusaui amplius.

quando te auratam et uestitam bene habet, ancillas, penum   [51

recte praehibet, melius sanam est, mulier, mentem sumere.

Ma. at ille suppilat mihi aurum et pallas ex arcis domo,

me despoliat, mea ornamenta clam ad meretrices degerit.

Se. male facit, si istuc facit ; si non facit, tu male facis   55

quae insontem insimules. *Ma.* quin etiam nunc habet pallam,
                                               pater,

⟨et⟩ spinter, quod ad hanc detulerat, nunc, quia resciui, refert

Se. iám ego ex hoc, ut factumst, scibo.   ⟨íbo⟩ ad hominem
                                     atque ⟨ad⟩loquar.

dic mihi istúc, Menaechme, quod uos dissertatis, ut sciam.

quid tu tristis es ? quid illa autem irata aps te destitit ?   60

Men. quisquis es, quidquid tibi nomen est, senex, summum
                                     Iouem

deosque do testis—   *Se.* qua de re aut quoius rei rerum
                                     omnium ?

Sen. He is wiser, because he cannot be quiet at home. 34

Mul. There he feasts and banquets, and spends, and spoils.

Sen. Would ye have your husband serve ye as your drudge? Ye will not let him make merry, nor entertain his friends at home.

Mul. Father, will ye take his part in these abuses, and forsake me?   40

Sen. Not so, daughter; but if I see cause, I will as well) tell him of his duty.

Men. Tra. [*aside*] I would I were gone from this prating father and daughter.

Sen. Hitherto I see not but he keeps ye well; ye [45 want nothing; apparel, money, servants, meat, drink, all things necessary. I fear there is fault in you.

Mul. But he filcheth away my apparel and my jewels, to give to his trulls.

Sen. If he doth so, 'tis very ill done: if not, you do [50 ill to say so.

Mul. You may believe me, father, for there you may see my cloak which now he hath fetched home again, and my chain which he stole from me.

Sen. Now will I go talk with him to know the [55 truth. [*To* Men. Tra.] Tell me, Menechmus, how is it that I hear such disorder in your life? Why are ye so sad, man? wherein hath your wife offended you?

Men. Tra. Old man (what to call ye I know not), by high Jove, and by all the gods I swear unto you, whatsoever this

Men. me neque isti male fecisse mulieri quae me arguit
hanc domo ab se surrupuisse atque apstulisse—*Ma.* deierat ?
Men. sí ego intra aedis huiius umquam ubi habitat penetraui [65
⟨pedem⟩,
omnium hominum exopto ut fiam miserorum miserrumus.
Se. sanun es qui istuc exoptes aut neges te umquam pedem
in eas aedis intulisse ubi habitas, insanissume ?
Men. tun, senex, ais habitare med in illisce aedibus ?
Se. tu negas ? *Men.* nego hercle uero. *Se.* immo hercle [70
inuere negas ;
nisi quo nocte hac exnigrasti. ⟨tu⟩ concede huc, filia.
quid tu ais ? num hinc exmigrastis ? *Ma.* quém in locum
aut ⟨quam⟩ ob rem, opsecro ?
Se. non edepol scio. *Ma.* profecto ludit te hic. non
tu[te] tenes ?
Se. iam uero, Menaechme, sati' iocatu's. nunc hanc rem
gere.
Men. quaeso, quid mihi tecum est ? unde aut quis tu homo [75
es ? *
tibi aut ádeo isti, quae mihi molestiaest quoquo modo ?
Ma. uiden tu illic oculos uirere ? ut uiridis exoritur colos
ex temporibus atque fronte, ut oculi scintillant, uide !
Men. quid mihi meliust quam, quando illi me insanire praedicant,
ego med adsimulem insanire, ut illos a me apsterream ?   80
Ma. ut pandiculans oscitatur ! quid nunc faciam, mi pater ?
Se. concede huc, mea nata, ab istoc quam potest longissume.

woman here accuseth me to have stolen from her, it is utterly
false and untrue ; and if ever I set foot within her doors, [62
I wish the greatest misery in the world to light upon me.

Sen. Why, fond man, art thou mad, to deny that thou ever
setst foot within thine own house where thou dwellest ?   65

Men. Tra. Do I dwell in that house ?

Sen. Dost thou deny it ?

Men. Tra. I do.

Sen. Hark ye, daughter; are ye removed out of your
house ?   70

Mul. Father, he useth you as he doth me : this life I have
with him.

Sen. Menechmus, I pray leave this fondness ; ye jest too
perversely with your friends.

Men. Tra. Good old father, what, I pray, have you to [75
do with me ? or why should this woman thus trouble me,
with whom I have no dealings in the world ?

Mul. Father, mark, I pray, how his eyes sparkle : they
roll in his head; his colour goes and comes; he looks
wildly. See, see.   80

Men. Tra. [*aside*] What ? they say now I am mad : the
best way for me is to feign myself mad indeed, so shall I be
rid of them.

Mul. Look how he stares about, how he gapes !

Sen. Come away, daughter : come from him.   85

Men. euhoe atque euhoe, Bromie, quo me in siluam uenatum

                            uocas?

audio, sed non abire possum ab his regionibus,

ita illa me ab laeua rabiosa femina adseruat canes,   85

poste autem illinc hircus †talus†, qui saepe aetate in sua

perdidit ciuem innocentem falso testimonio.

Se. uae capiti tuo!   *Men.* ecce, Apollo mihi ex oraclo

                          imperat

ut ego illic oculos exuram lampadi[bu]s ardentibus.

Ma. perii! mi pater, minatur mihi oculos exurere.   90

Men. ei mihi! insanire me aiunt, ultro quom ipsi insaniunt.

Se. filia, heus!   *Ma.* quid est? quid agimus?   *Se.* quid si

                    ego huc seruos cito?

ibo, abducam qui hunc hinc tollant et domi deuinciant

priu' quam turbarum quid faciat ampliús.   *Men.* enim haereo;

ni occupo aliquid mihi consilium, hí domum me ad se [95

                          auferent.

pugnis me uotas in huiius ore quicquam parcere,

nei a meis oculis apscedat in malam magnam crucem.

faciam quod iubes, Apollo.   *Se.* fuge domum quantum

                          potest,

ne hic te optundat.   *Ma.* fugio. amabo, ádserua istunc, mi

                          pater,

ne quo hinc abeat. sumne ego mulier misera quae illaec [100

                          audio?—

Men. hau male illánc amoui; (amoueo) nunc hunc inpuris-

                          sumum

Men. Tra. Bacchus, Apollo, Phœbus,do ye call me to come
hunt in the woods with you? I see, I hear, I come, I fly;
but I cannot get out of these fields. Here is an old mastiff
bitch stands barking at me; and by her stands an old goat
that bears false witness against many a poor man.   90

Sen. Out upon him, Bedlam fool.

Men. Tra. Hark, Apollo commands me that I should rend
out her eyes with a burning lamp.

Mul. O father, he threatens to pull out mine eyes.

Men. Tra. Good gods, these folk say I am mad, [95
and doubtless they are mad themselves.

Sen. Daughter.

Mul. Here, father: what shall we do?

Sen. What if I fetch my folks hither, and have him
carried in before he do any harm?   100

Men. [*aside*] How now? they will carry me in if I look
not to myself: I were best to scare them better yet.
[*Aloud*] Dost thou bid me, Phœbus, to tear this dog in
pieces with my nails? If I lay hold on him, I will do thy
commandment.   105

Sen. Get thee into thy house, daughter; away quickly.

                                        [*Exit* Mul.]

Men. She is gone: yea, Apollo, I will sacrifice this old

barbatum, tremulum Titanum, qui cluet Cygno patre.
ita mihi imperas ut ego huius membra atque ossa atque artua
comminuam illo scipione quem ipse habet. *Se.* dabitur
malum,

me quidem si attigeris aut si propius ad me accesseris.   105
Men. faciam quod iubes ; securim capiam ancipitem atque
hunc senem

osse fini dedolabo ássulatim uiscera.

Se. enim uero illud praecauendumst atque adcurandumst mihi ;
sane ego illúm metuo, ut minatur, ne quid male faxit mihi.
Men. multa mi imperas, Apollo : nunc equos iunctos iubes [110
capere me indomitos, ferocis, atque in currum inscendere,
ut ego hunc proteram leonem uetulum, olentem, edentulum.
iam astiti in currum, iam lora teneo, iam stimulum : in
manust.

agite equi, facitote sonitus ungularum appareat,
cursu celeri facite inflexa sit pedum pernicitas.   115
Se. mihin equis iunctis minare ?   *Men.* écce, Apollo, denuo
me iubes facere impetum in eum qui stat atque occidere.
sed quis hic est qui me capillo hínc de curru deripit ?
imperium tuom demutat atque edictum Apollinis.

  Se. eu hercle morbum acrem ac durum ! * * *   120
*   *   * di, uostram fidem !
uel hic qui insanit quam ualuit paullo prius !
ei derepente tantus morbus incidit.
eibo atque accersam medicum iam quantum potest.—

beast unto thee ; and if thou commandest me, I will cut his throat with that dagger that hangs at his girdle.

Sen. Come not near me, sirrah.   110

Men. Yea, I will quarter him, and pull all the bones out of his flesh, and then will I barrel up his bowels.

Sen. Sure, I am sore afraid he will do some hurt.   113

Men. Tra. Many things thou commandest me, Apollo : wouldst thou have me harness up these wild horses, and then climb up into the chariot, and so over-ride this old stinking toothless lion ?   So now I am in the chariot, and I have hold on the reins : here is my whip.   Hait ! come, ye wild jades, make a hideous noise with your stamping : hait, I say : will ye not go ?   120

Sen. What ? doth he threaten me with his horses ?

Men Tra. Hark ! now Apollo bids me ride over him that stands there, and kill him.   How now ? who pulls me down from my chariot by the hairs of my head ? Oh, shall I not fulfil Apollo's commandment?   125

Sen. See, see, what a sharp disease this is, and how well he was even now.   I will fetch a physician straight, before he grow too far into this rage.   *Exit.*

Scaena III

Menaechmvs II. Senex.

Men. Iamne isti abierunt, quaeso, ex conspectu meo,
qui me ui cogunt ut ualidus insaniam ?
quid cesso abire ad nauem dum saluo licet ?
uosque omnis quaeso, si senex reuenerit,
ni me indicetis qua platea hinc aufugerim.—— 5
Se. lumbi sedendo, óculi spectando dolent,
manendo medicum dum se ex opere recipiat.
odiosus tandem uix ab aegrotis uenit,
ait se óbligasse crus fractum Aesculapio,
Apollini autem bracchium. nunc cogito 10
utrum me dicam ducere medicum an fabrum.
atque eccum incedit. moue formicinum gradum.

Scaena IV

Medicvs. Senex.

Med. Quid esse ílli morbi dixeras ? narra, senex.
num laruatust aut cerritus ? fac sciam.
num eum ueternus aut aqua intercus tenet ?
Se. quin ea te caussa duco ut id dicas mihi
atque illum ut sanum facias. *Med.* perfacile id quidems : 5
sanum futurum, mea ego id promitto fide.
Se. magna cum cura ego illum curari uolo.

Scene III

Men. Tra. Are they both gone now? I'll then hie me away to my ship: 'tis time to be gone from hence. *Exit.* [130

Sen. My loins ache with sitting, and mine eyes with looking, while I stay for yonder lazy physician: see now where the creeping drawlatch comes.

Scene IV

Enter Senex *and* Medicus.

Med. What disease hath he, said you? Is it a letharge or a lunacy, or melancholy, or dropsy?

Sen. Wherefor, I pray, do I bring you, but that you should tell me what it is, and cure him of it?

Med. quin suspirabo plus †sescenta† in dies :
ita ego éum cum cura magna curabo tibi.   9
Se. atque eccum ipsum hominem. ópseruemus quam rem
                                                    agat.

Scaena V

Menaechmvs I.   Senex.   Medicvs.

Men. Edepol ne hic dies peruorsus atque aduorsus mi optigit
quae me clam ratus sum facere, ómnia ea fecit palam
parasitus qui me compleuit flagiti et formidinis,
meus Vlixes, suo qui regi tantum conciuit mali.
quém ego hóminem, si quidem uiuo, uita euoluam sua—   5
sed ego stultus sum, qui illius esse dico quae meast :
meo cibo et sumptu educatust.   anima priuabo uirum.
condigne autem haec meretrix fecit, ut mos est meretricius :
quia rogo palla ut referatur rusum ad uxorem meam,   9
mihi se ait dedisse. eu edepol ! né ego homo uiuo miser.
Se. audin quae loquitur ?   *Med.* se miserum praedicat.
                                       Se. adeas uelim.
Med. saluos sis, Menaechme. quaeso, qur apertas brac-
                                              chium ?
non tu scis quantum isti morbo nunc tuo facias mali ?
Men. quin tu te suspendis ? *Se.* ecquid sentis ? *Med.* quidni
                                           sentiam ?
non potest haec res ellebori iungere optinerier.   15
sed quid ais, Menaechme ? *Men.* quid uis ? *Med.* dic mihi
                                    hoc quod te rogo

Med. Fie, make no question of that. I'll cure him, I   [5
warrant ye.   Oh, here he comes.   Stay, let us mark what
he doth.   [*They stand apart.*]

Scene V

Enter Menechmus *the Citizen.*

Men. Cit. Never in my life had I more overthwart fortune
in one day, and all by the villainy of this false knave the
Parasite, my Ulysses that works such mischiefs against me his
king.   But let me live no longer but I'll be revenged upon
the life of him.   His life? nay, 'tis my life, for he lives   [5
by my meat and drink.   I'll utterly withdraw the slave's life
from him.   And Erotium she plainly sheweth what she is;
who because I require the cloak again to carry to my wife,
saith I gave it her, and flatly falls out with me.   How
unfortunate am I!   10

Sen. [*aside to* Med.] Do ye hear him?

Med. [*aside to* Sen.] He complains of his fortune.

Sen. [*aside to* Med.] Go to him.

Med. Menechmus, how do ye, man?   Why keep you
not your cloak over your arm?   It is very hurtful to your
disease.   Keep ye warm, I pray.   16

Men. Cit. Why, hang thyself, what carest thou?

Med. Sir, can you smell anything?

Men. Cit. I smell a prating dolt of thee.   19

album an atrum unium potas ?   *Men.* quin tu is in malam
crucem ?
Med. iam hercle occeptat insanire primulum.   *Men.* quín
[tu] me interrogas
purpureum panem an puniceum soleam ego esse an luteum ?
soleamne esse auis squamossas, piscis pennatos ?   *Se.* papae !
audin tu ut deliramenta loquitur ? quid cessas dare   21
potionis aliquid priu' quam percipit insania ?
Med. mane modo, etiam percontabor alia.   *Se.* occidis
fabulans.
Med. dic mihi hoc : solent tibi umquam óculi duri fieri ? 24
Men. quid ? tu me locustam censes esse, homo ignauissume ?
Med. dic mihi : enumquam intestina tibi crepant, quod
sentias ?
Men. ubi satur sum, nulla crepitant ; quando essurio, tum
crepant.
Med. hoc quidem edepol hau pro insano uerbum respondit
mihi.
perdormiscin usque ad lucem ? facilin tu dormis cubans ?
Men. perdormisco, si resolui árgentum quoi debeo—   30
qui te Iuppiter dique omnes, percontator, perduint !
Med. nunc homo insanire occeptat : de illis uerbis caue tibi.
Se. immo Nestor nunc quidem est de uerbis, praeut dudum
fuit :
nam dudum uxorem suam esse aiebat rabiosam canem.   34
Men. quid, ego ? *Se.* dixti insanus, inquam.   *Men.* égone ?
Se. tú istic, qui mihi

Med. Oh, I will have your head throughly purged. Pray tell me, Menechmus, what use you to drink? white wine, or claret?

Men. Cit. What the devil carest thou?

Sen. [*aside to* Med.] Look, his fit now begins.   24

Men. Cit. Why dost not as well ask me whether I eat bread, or cheese, or beef, or porridge, or birds that bear feathers, or fishes that have fins?

Sen. [*aside to* Med.] See what idle talk he falleth into.

Med. [*aside to* Sen.] Tarry; I will ask him further. [*To* Men. Cit.] Menechmus, tell me, be not your eyes heavy and dull sometimes?   31

Men. Cit. What, dost think I am an owl?

Med. Do not your guts gripe ye, and croak in your belly?

Men. Cit. When I am hungry they do, else not.

Med. He speaks not like a madman in that. Sleep ye soundly all night?   36

Men Cit. When I have paid my debts I do. The mischief light on thee, with all thy frivolous questions!

Med. Oh, now he rageth upon those words: take heed.

Sen. Oh, this is nothing to the rage he was in even now. He called his wife bitch, and all to nought.   41

Men. Cit. Did I?

Sen. Thou did'st, mad fellow, and threatened'st to ride

etiam me iunctis quadrigis minitatu's prosternere.
egomet haec te uidi facere, égomet haec ted arguo.
Men. at ego te sacram coronam surrupuisse Ioui' ⟨scio⟩,
et ob eam rem in carcerem ted esse compactum scio,
et postquam es emissus, caesum uirgis sub furca scio ;   40
tum patrem occidisse et matrem uendidisse etiam scio.
satin haec pro sano male dicta male dictis respondeo ?
Se. opsecro hercle, medice, propere quidquid facturu's face.
non uides hominem insanire ? *Med.* scin quid facias [44
                                          optumum est ?
ad me face uti deferatur. *Se.* itane censes ? *Med.* quippini ?
ibi meo arbitratu potero curare hominem. *Se.* age ut lubet.
Med. elleborum potabis faxo áliquos uiginti dies.
Men. at ego te pendentem fodiam stimulis triginta dies.
Med. i, arcesse homines qui illunc ad me deferant. *Se.* quot
                                          sunt satis ?
Med. proinde ut insanire uideo, quattuor, nihilo minus.   50
Se. iám hic erunt. adserua tu istunc, medice. *Med.* immo
                                          ibo domum,
ut parentur quibu' paratis opus est. tu seruos iube
hunc ad me ferant. *Se.* iam ego illic faxo erit. *Med.*
                                abeo.—— *Se.* uale.——
Men. abiit socerus, abit medicús. nunc solus sum. pro
                                      Iuppiter !
quid illuc est quod med hisce homines insanire praedicant ? 55
nam equidem, postquam gnatus sum, numquam aegrotaui
                                        unum diem

over me here with a chariot and horses, and to kill me, and
tear me in pieces. This thou did'st : I know what I say. 45

Men. Cit. I say, thou stolest Jupiter's crown from his
head, and thou wert whipped through the town for it, and
that thou hast killed thy father, and beaten thy mother.   Do
ye think that I am so mad that I cannot devise as notable
lies of you as you do of me?   50

Sen. Master Doctor, pray heartily make speed to cure him.
See you not how mad he waxeth?

Med. I'll tell ye, he shall be brought over to my house,
and there I will cure him.

Sen. Is that best?   55

Med. What else?   There I can order him as I list.

Sen. Well, it shall be so.

Med. Oh, sir, I will make you take neesing powder this
twenty days.

Men. Cit. I'll beat ye first with a bastinado this thirty
days.   61

Med. Fetch men to carry him to my house.

Sen. How many will serve the turn?

Med. Being no madder than he is now, four will serve.   64

Sen. I'll fetch them.   Stay you with him, Master Doctor.

Med. No, by my faith : I'll go home to make ready all
things needful.   Let your men bring him hither.

Sen. I go.   *Exeunt* [Sen. *and* Med.].

Men. Cit. Are they both gone?   Good gods, what
meaneth this?   These men say I am mad, who without [70

H

neque ego insanio neque pugnas neque ego litis coepio.
saluos saluos alios uideo, noui ⟨ego⟩ homines, adloquor
an illi perperam insanire me aiunt, ipsi insaniunt?
quid ego nunc faciam? domum ire cupio : úxor non sinit ; 60
huc autem nemo intromittit.   nimi' prouentum est nequiter.
hic ero usque ; ad noctem saltem, credo, intromittar domum.

SCAENA VI

MESSENIO.

Mes. Spectamen bono seruo id est, qui rem erilem
procurat, uidet, conlocat cogitatque,
   ut apsente ero rem eri diligenter
      tutetur quam si ipse adsit aut rectius.
   tergum quam gulam, crura quam uentrem oportet   5
      potiora esse quoi cor modeste situmst.
         recordétur id, qui nihili sunt, quid eis preti
detur ab suis eris, ignauis, inprobis uiris :
            uerbera, compedes,
   molae, [magna] lassitudo, fames, frigu' durum,   10
         haec pretia sunt ignauiae.
id ego male malum métuo : propterea bonum esse certumst
                                                     potius
quam malum ; nám magi' multo patior faciliu' uerba : uerbera
                                                     ego odi,
nimioque edo lubentius molitum quam molitum praehibeo.

doubt are mad themselves. I stir not, I fight not, I am

not sick. I speak to them, I know them. Well, what

were I now best to do? I would go home, but my wife

shuts me forth a doors. Erotium is far out with me too.

Even here I will rest me till the evening: I hope by [75

that time, they will take pity on me. [*Seats himself apart.*]

SCENE VI

Enter MESSENIO, *the Traveller's servant,* [*and*

another servant].

* *Mess.* The proof of a good servant, is to regard his

master's business as well in his absence as in his presence; and

I think him a very fool that is not careful as well for his ribs

and shoulders, as for his belly and throat. When I think upon

the rewards of a sluggard, I am ever pricked with a [5

careful regard of my back and shoulders; for in truth I have

no fancy to these blows, as many a one hath. Methinks it is

H 2

propterea eri imperium exsequor, bene et sedate seruo id ;
atque id mihi prodest.   16

alii sei ita ut in rem esse ducunt sint, ego ita ero ut me esse
oportet ;

metum id míhi adhibeam, culpam apstineám, ero ut
omnibus in locis sim praesto :

serui qui quom culpa carent metuont i solent esse eris
utibiles.

nam illi qui nil metuont, postquam malum †promeri- ⌈20
tumque† ei metuont.

metuam hau multum. prope est quando †ceruso faciam†
pretium exsoluet.

⟨eo⟩ ego exemplo seruio, tergo ut in rem esse arbitror.

postquam in tabernam uassa et seruos conlocaui, ut iusserat,

ita uenio aduorsum. nunc fores pultabo, adesse ut me sciat,

†neque utrum† ex hoc saltu damni saluom ut educam foras.

sed metuo ne sero ueniam depugnato proelio.   26

Scaena VII

Senex. Menaechmvs I. Messenio. Lorarii.

Se. Per ego uobis deos atque homines dico ut imperium
meum

sapienter habeatis curae, quae ímperaui atque impero :

facite illic homo iam in medicinam ablatus sublimen siet,

nisi quidem uos uostra crura aut latera nihili penditis.

caue quisquam quod illíc minitetur uostrum flocci fecerit.   5

no pleasure to a man to be basted with a rope's end two or three hours together.   I have provided yonder in the town for all our mariners, and safely bestowed all my master's [10 trunks and fardels ; and am now coming to see if he be yet got forth of this dangerous gulf, where I fear me he is overplunged.   Pray God he be not overwhelmed and past help ere I come.

SCENE VII

Enter SENEX, *with four Lorarii, Porters.*

Sen. Before gods and men, I charge and command you, sirs, to execute with great care that which I appoint you : if ye love the safety of your own ribs and shoulders, then go take me up my son-in-law, lay all hands upon him : why

quid statis ? quid dubitatis ? iam sublimen raptum oportuit.
ego ibo ad medicum : praesto ero illi, quom uenietis.

Men. occidi !

quid hoc ést negoti ? quid illisce homines ad me currunt,
opsecro ?

quid uoltis uos ? quid quaeritatis ? quid me circumsistitis ?
quo rapitis me ? quo fertis me ? perii, opsecro uostram fidem,
[10

Epidamnienses, subuenite, ciues ! quin me mittitis ?
Mes. pro di inmortales ! opsecro, quid ego oculis aspicio
meis ?

erum meum indignissume nescioqui sublimen ferunt.
Men. ecquis suppetias mi audet ferre ? *Mes.* égo, ere,
aúdacissume.

o facinus indignum et malúm, Epidamnii ciues, erum   15
meum hic in pacato oppido luci deripier in uia,
qui liber ad uos uenerit !

mittite istunc.   *Men.* opsecro te, quisquis es, operam mihi ut
des

neu sinas in me insignite fieri tantam iniuriam.
Mes. immo et operam dabo et defendam et subuenibo sedulo. 20
numquam te patiar perire, me perirest aequius.
eripe oculum istic, ab umero qui tenet, ere, te opsecro.
hisce ego iam sementem in ore faciam pugnosque opseram.
maxumo hodie malo hercle uostro ístunc fertis.   mittite.
Men. teneo ego huic oculum.   *Mes.* face ut oculi locus in [25
capite appareat.

stand ye still? what do ye doubt? I say, care not for his [5
threatenings, nor for any of his words. Take him up, and
bring him to the Physician's house : I will go thither before.

Exit. [*The Porters sieze* Men.]

Men. Cit. What news? how now, masters? what will ye
do with me? why do ye thus beset me? whither carry ye
me? Help, help, neighbours, friends, citizens !   10

Mess. O Jupiter, what do I see? my master abused by a
company of varlets.

Men. Cit. Is there no good man will help me?

Mess. Help ye, master? yes, the villains shall have my life
before they shall thus wrong ye. 'Tis more fit, I should [15
be killed, than you thus handled. Pull out that rascal's eye
that holds ye about the neck there. I'll clout these peasants ;
out, ye rogue ; let go, ye varlet.

Men. Cit. I have hold of this villain's eye.

Mess. Pull it out, and let the place appear in his head.
Away ye cut-throat thieves, ye murtherers.   21

uos scelesti, uos rapaces, uos praedones!   *Lo.* periimus!
opsecro hercle!   *Mes.* mittite ergo.   *Men.* quid me uobis
tactiost?

pecte pugnis.   *Mes.* agite abite, fugite hinc in malam crucem
em tibi etiam! quia postremus cedis, hoc praemi feres.
nimi' bene ora commetaui atque ex mea sententia.   30
edepol, ere, ne tibi suppetias temperi adueni modo.
Men. at tibi di semper, adulescens, quisquis es, faciant bene.
nam apsque ted ésset, hodie numquam ad solem occasum
uiuerem.

Mes. ergo edepol, si recte facias, ere, med emittas manu.
Men. liberem ego te?   *Mes.* uerum, quandoquidem, ere, [35
te seruaui.   *Men.* quid est?

adulescens, erras.   *Mes.* quid, erro?   *Men.* per Iouem
adiuro patrem,

med erum tuom non esse.   *Mes.* non taces?   *Men.* non
mentior;

nec meu' seruos numquam tale fecit quale tu mihi.
Mes. sic sine igitur si tuom negas me ésse, abire liberum.
Med. mea quidem hercle caussa liber esto atque ito quo uoles.
[40

Mes. nemp' iubes?   *Men.* iubeo hercle, si quid imperi est in
te mihi.

Mes. salue, mi patrone. 'quom tu liber es, Messenio,
gaudeo.' credo hercle uobis. sed, patrone, te opsecro,
ne minus imperes mihi quam quom tuos seruos fui.
apud ted habitabo et quando ibis, una tecum ibo domum.   45

Lo. Omnes. Oh, oh, ay !   [*Cry pitifully.*]

Mess. Away, get ye hence, ye mongrels, ye dogs. Will ye be gone? Thou rascal behind there, I'll give thee somewhat more, take that. [*Exeunt* Lorarii.] It was [25 time to come, master ; you had been in good case, if I had not been here now.   I told you what would come of it.

Men. Cit. Now as the gods love me, my good friend, I thank thee : thou hast done that for me which I shall never be able to requite.   30

Mess. I'll tell ye how, sir ; give me my freedom.

Men. Cit. Should I give it thee ?

Mess. Seeing you cannot requite my good turn.

Men. Cit. Thou art deceived, man.

Mess. Wherein?   35

Men. Cit. On mine honesty, I am none of thy master ; I had never yet any servant would do so much for me.

Mess. Why then bid me be free : will you?

Men. Cit. Yea, surely : be free, for my part.

Mess. Oh, sweetly spoken; thanks, my good master. 40

Servus alius. Messenio, we are all glad of your good fortune.

Mess. Oh, master, I'll call ye master still. I pray use me in any service as ye did before. I'll dwell with you still ; and when ye go home, I'll wait upon you.   45

Men. Cit. Nay, nay, it shall not need.

Men. minime.   *Mes.* nunc ibo in tabernam, uassa atque
                                                    argentum tibi
referam.   recte est opsignatum in uidulo marsuppium
cum uiatico : id tibi iam huc adferam.   *Men.* adfer strenue.
Mes. saluom tibi ita ut mihi dedisti reddibó.   hic me mane.—
Men. nimia mira mihi quidem hodie exorta sunt miris modis: 50
alii me negant eum esse qui sum atque excludunt foras ;
etiam hic seruom se meum esse aiebat quem ego emisi manu,
[uel ille qui se petere argentum modo, qui seruom se meum
esse aiebat, ⟨med erum suom⟩, quem ego modo emisi manu]
is ait se mihi adlaturum cum argento marsuppium :   55
id si attulerit, dicam ut a me ábeat liber quo uolet,
ne tum, quando sanus factus sit, a me argentum petat.
socer et medicus me insanire aiebant.   quid sit mira sunt.
haec nihilo esse mihi uidentur setius quam somnia.
nunc ibo intro ad hanc meretricem, quamquam suscenset [60
                                                    mihi,
si possum exorare ut pallam reddat quam referam domum.—

SCAENA VIII

MENAECHMVS II.   MESSENIO.

Men. Men hodie usquam conuenisse te, audax, audes dicere,
postquam aduorsum mi imperaui ut huc uenires ?   *Mes.* quin
                                                    modo
erupui, homines qui ferebant te sublimen quattuor,

Mess. I'll go straight to the Inn, and deliver up my accounts, and all your stuff. Your purse is locked up safely sealed in the casket, as you gave it me. I will go fetch it to you.   50

Men. Cit. Do, fetch it.

Mess. I will.   [*Exit.*]

Men. Cit. I was never thus perplexed. Some deny me to be him that I am, and shut me out of their doors. This fellow saith he is my bondman, and of me he begs his [55 freedom: he will fetch my purse and money. Well, if he bring it, I will receive it, and set him free. I would he would so go his way. My old father-in-law and the doctor say I am mad. Whoever saw such strange demeanours? Well, though Erotium be never so angry, yet once [60 again I'll go see if by entreaty I can get the cloak on her to carry to my wife.   *Exit.*

Scene VIII

Enter Menechmus *the Traveller, and* Messenio.

Men. Tra. Impudent knave, wilt thou say that I ever saw thee since I sent thee away to-day, and bade thee come for me after dinner?

Mess. Ye make me stark mad: I took ye away, and rescued ye from four great big-boned villains, that were [5

apud hasce aedis. tu clamabas deum fidem atque hominum
omnium,
quom ego accurro teque eripio ui, pugnando, ingratiis.   5
ob eam rem, quia te seruaui, me amisisti liberum.
quom argentum dixi me petere et uasa, tu quantum potest
praecucurristi obuiam, ut quae fecisti infitias eas.
Men. liberum ego te iussi abire? *Mes.* certo. *Men.* quin
certissumumst
mepte potius fieri seruom quam te umquam emittam manu. 10

Menaechmvs I. Messenio.
Menaechmvs II.

Men.[1] Si uoltis per oculos iurare, nihilo hercle ea caussa
magis
facietis ut ego hódie apstulerim pallam et spinter, pessumae.
Mes. pro di inmortales! quid ego uideo? *Men.*[2] quid
uides? *Mes.* speculum tuom.
Men.[2] quid negoti est? *Mes.* tuast imago. tam consimilest
quam potest.
Men.[2] pol profecto haud est dissimilis, meam quom formam
noscito. [5
Men.[1] o adulescens, salue, qui me seruauisti, quisquis es.
Mes. adulescens, quaeso hercle eloquere tuom mihi nomen,
nisi piget
Men.[1] non edepol ita promeruisti de me ut pigeat quae uelis

carrying ye away even here in this place. Here they had
ye up ; you cried Help, help ! I came running to you : you
and I together beat them away by main force. Then for
my good turn and faithful service, ye gave me my freedom : I told ye I would go fetch your casket : now in [10
the meantime you ran some other way to get before me, and
so you deny it all again.

Men. Tra. I gave thee thy freedom?

Mess. You did.

Men. Tra. When I give thee thy freedom, I'll be a
bondman myself; go thy ways.   16

Mess. Whew, marry, I thank you for nothing.

Enter MENECHMUS *the Citizen,* [*talking back to* EROTIUM *and
her maid within*].

Men. Cit. Forsworn queans, swear till your hearts ache,
and your eyes fall out, ye shall never make me believe that I
carried hence either cloak or chain.   20

Mess. Oh, heavens, master, what do I see?

Men. Tra. What?

Mess. Your ghost.

Men. Tra. What ghost?

Mess. Your image, as like you as can be possible.   25

Men. Tra. [*looking at* Men. Cit.] Surely not much unlike
me, as I think.

Men. Cit. O my good friend and helper, well met: thanks
for thy late good help.

Mess. Sir, may I crave to know your name?   30

⟨opsequi⟩. mihi est Menaechmo nomen. *Men.*[2] immo ede-
　　　　　　　　　　　　　　　　　　　pol mihi.
Men.[1] Siculus sum Syracusanus. *Men.*[2] ea domus et [10
　　　　　　　　　　　　　　　　　　patria est mihi.
Men.[1] quid ego ex te audio ? *Men.*[2] hoc quod res est.
　　　　　　　Mes. noui equidem hunc : erus est meus.
egoquidem huiius seruos sum, sed med esse huiius credidi.
ego hunc censebam ted esse, huic etiam exhibui negotium.
quaeso ignoscas si quid stulte dixi atque inprudens tibi.
Men.[2] delirare mihi uidere : non commeministi semul　15
te hodie mecum exire ex naui ? *Mes.* énim uero aequom
　　　　　　　　　　　　　　　　　　postulas.
tú erus es : tu seruoni quaere. tu salueto : tu uale.
hunc ego esse aio Menaechmum. *Men.*[1] át ego me. *Men.*[2]
　　　　　　　　　　　　　　　　quae haec fabulast ?
tú es Menaechmus ? *Men.*[1] me esse dico, Moscho prognatum
　　　　　　　　　　　　　　　　　　　patre.
Men.[2] tun meo patre es prognatus ? *Men.*[1] immo equidem, [20
　　　　　　　　　　　　　　　　adulescens, meo ;
tuom tibi neque occupare neque praeripere postulo.
Mes. di inmortales, spem insperatam date mihi quam suspico !
nam, nisi me animus fallit, hi sunt geminei germanei duo.
nam et patrem et patriam commemorant pariter quae fuerint
　　　　　　　　　　　　　　　　　　　sibi.
seuocabo erum. Menaechme. *Men.*[1] *Men.*[2] quid uis ? [25
　　　　　　　　　　　　　　Mes. non ambos uolo,
sed uter uostrorum est aduectus mecum naui, *Men.*[1] non ego.

Men. Cit. I were to blame if I should not tell thee anything; my name is Menechmus.

Men. Tra. Nay, my friend, that is my name.

Men. Cit. I am of Syracusis in Sicilia.

Men. Tra. So am I.   35

Mess. Are you a Syracusan?

Men. Cit. I am.

Mess. Oho, I know ye: this is my master: I thought he
there had been my master, and was proffering my service to
him. Pray pardon me, sir, if I said anything I should not.   40

Men. Tra. Why, doting patch, didst thou not come with
me this morning from the ship?

Mess. My faith, he says true. This is my master, you
may go look ye a man. God save ye, master: you sir,
farewell. This is Menechmus.   45

Men. Cit. I say, that I am Menechmus.

Mess. What a jest is this? Are you Menechmus?

Men. Cit. Even Menechmus, the son of Moschus.

Men. Tra. My father's son?

Men. Cit. Friend, I go about neither to take your father
nor your country from you.   51

Mess. [*aside*] Oh, immortal gods, let it fall out as I hope;
and for my life these two are the two twins, all things agree
to jump together. I will speak to my master. Menechmus.

Both. What wilt thou?   55

Mess. I call you not both: but which of you came with
me from the ship?

Men. at ego.   *Mes.* te uolo igitur. huc concede.   *Men.*²
                                       concessi.   quid est
Mes. illic hómo aut sycophanta aut geminus est frater tuos.
nam ego hominem hominis similiorem numquam uidi alterum.
neque aqua aquae nec lacte est lactis, crede mi, usquam [30
                                           similius
quam hic tui est, tuque huiius autem ; poste eandem patriam
                                          ac patrem
memorat.   meliust nos adire átque hunc percontarier.
*Men.*² hercle qui tu me admonuisti recte et habeo gratiam.
perge operam dare, opsecro hercle ; liber esto, si inuenis
hunc meum fratrem esse.   *Mes.* spero.   *Men.*² et ego [35
                                      idem spero fore.
Mes. quid ais tu ? Menaechmum, opinor, te uocari dixeras.
*Men.*¹ ita uero.   *Mes.* huic item Menaechmo nomen est.
                                        in Sicilia
te Syracusis natum esse dixisti : hic natust ibi.
Moschum tibi patrem fuisse dixti : huíc itidem fuit.
nunc operam potestis ambo mihi dare et uobis simul.   40
*Men.*¹ promeruisti ut ne quid ores quod uelis quin impetres.
tam quasi me emeris argento, liber seruibo tibi.
Mes. spes mihi est uos inuenturum fratres germanos duos
geminos, una matre natos et patre uno uno die.   44
*Men.*¹ mira memoras.   utinam ecficere quod pollicitu's possies.
Mes. possum.   sed nunc agite uterque id quod rogabo
                                         ditice.
*Men.*¹ ubi lubet, roga : réspondebo.   nil reticebo quod sciam.

Men. Cit. Not I.

Men. Tra. I did.

Mess. Then I call you. Come hither. 60

Men. Tra. What's the matter?

Mess. [*aside to* Men. Tra.] This same is either some notable cozening juggler, or else it is your brother whom we seek. I never saw one man so like another: water to water, nor milk to milk, is not liker than he is to you. 65

Men. Tra. [*aside to* Mess.] Indeed I think thou sayest true. Find it that he is my brother, and I here promise thee thy freedom.

Mess. [*aside to* Men. Tra.] Well, let me about it. [*To* Men. Cit.] Hear ye, sir; you say your name is [70 Menechmus.

Men. Cit. I do.

Mess. So is this man's. You are of Syracusis?

Men. Cit. True.

Mess. So is he. Moschus was your father? 75

Men. Cit. He was.

Mess. So was he his. What will you say, if I find that ye are brethren and twins?

Men. Cit. I would think it happy news.

Mess. Nay stay, masters both: I mean to have the honour of this exploit. Answer me: your name is Menechmus? 81

I

Mes. est tibi nomen Menaechmo ?   *Men.*[1] fateor.   *Mes.* est
itidem tibi ?

Men.[2] est.   *Mes.* patrem fuisse Moschum tibi ais ? *Men.*[1] ita
uero.   *Men.*[2] et mihi.

Mes. esne tu Syracusanus ? *Men.*[1] certo. *Mes.* quid tu ? [50
Men.[2] quippini ?

Mes. optume usque adhuc conueniunt signa. porro operam
date.

quid longissume meministi, dic mihi, in patria tua ?

Men.[1] cum patre ut abii Tarentum ád mercatum, postea

inter homines me deerrare á patre atque inde auehi.

Men.[2] Iuppiter supreme, serua me !   *Mes.* quid clamas? 55
quin taces ?

quot eras annos gnatus quom te pater a patria | auehit ?

Men.[1] septuennis : nam tunc dentes mihi cadebant primulum.

neque patrem numquam postilla uidi. *Mes.* quid? uos tum
patri

filii quot eratis ?   *Men.*[1] ut nunc maxume memini, duo.

Mes. uter eratis, tun an ille, maior ? *Men.*[1] aeque ambo [60
pares.

Mes. quí id potest ? *Men.*[1] geminei ambo eramus. *Men.*[2]
di me seruatum uolunt.

Mes. si interpellas, ego tacebo. *Men.*[2] potius taceo. *Mes.*
dic mihi :

uno nomine ambo eratis ? *Men.*[1] minime. nam mihi hoc erat,

quod nunc est, Menaechmo : íllum tum uocabant Sosiclem.

Men.[2] signa adgnoui, contineri quin complectar non queo. 65

Men. Cit. Yea.

Mess. And yours?

Men. Tra. And mine.

Mess. You are of Syracusis? 85

Men Cit. I am.

Men. Tra. And I.

Mess. Well, this goeth right thus far. What is the farthest thing that you remember there?

Men. Cit. How I went with my father to Tarentum, to a great mart, and there in the press I was stolen from him. 91

Men. Tra. O Jupiter!

Mess. [*to* Men. Tra.] Peace, what exclaiming is this? [*To* Men. Cit.] How old were ye then? 94

Men. Cit. About seven year old : for even then I shed teeth, and since that time I never heard of any of my kindred.

Mess. Had ye never a brother?

Men. Cit. Yes, as I remember, I heard them say, we were two twins. 100

Men. Tra. Oh, Fortune!

Mess. Tush, can ye not be quiet? Were ye both of one name?

Men. Cit. Nay, as I think, they called my brother, Sosicles. 105

Men. Tra. It is he. What need further proof? Oh, brother, brother, let me embrace thee!

I 2

mi germáne, gemine frater, salue.   ego sum Sosicles.

Men.[1] quo modo igitur post Menaechmo nomen est factum
tibi ?

Men.[2] postquam ad nos renuntiatum est te ✳ ✳ ✳ ✳
✳ ✳ ✳ ✳ ✳ ✳ ✳ ✳ et patrem esse mortuom,
auo' noster mutauit : quod tibi nomen est, fecit mihi.   70
Men.[1] credo ita esse factum ut dicis.   sed mih noc résponde.
Men.[2] roga.

Men.[1] quid erat nomen nostrae matri ?   *Men.*[2] Teuximarchae.
Men.[1] conuenit.

o salue, insperate, ánnis multis post quem conspicor.
Men.[2] frater, et tu, quém ego multeis miserieis, laboribus
usque adhuc quaesiui quemque ego esse inuentum gaudeo. 75
Mes. hoc erat quod haec te meretrix huius uocabat nomine :
hunc censebat te esse, credo, quom uocat te ad prandium.
Men.[1] namque edepol iussi hic mihi hodie prandium appa-
rarier,

clam meam uxorem, quoi pallam surrupui dudum domo,
eam dedi huic.   *Men.*[2] hanc, dicis, frater, pallam quam ego [80
habeo ?   *Men.*[1] ⟨haec east⟩.

quo modo haec ad te peruenit ?   *Men.*[1] meretrix huc ad
prandium

me abduxit, me sibi dedisse aiebat.   prandi perbene
potaui atque accubui scortum, pallam et aurum hoc ⟨apstuli⟩.
Men.[1] gaudeo edepol si quid propter me tibi euenit boni.
nam illa quom te ad se uocabat, memet esse credidit.   85
Mes. numquid me morare quin ego liber, ut iusti, siem ?

Men. Cit. Sir, if this be true, I am wonderfully glad : but how is it that ye are called Menechmus?   109

Men. Tra. When it was told us that you and our father were both dead, our grandsire, in memory of my father's name, changed mine to Menechmus.

Men. Cit. 'Tis very like he would do so indeed.   But let me ask ye one question more : what was our mother's name ?

Men. Tra. Theusimarche.   115

Men. Cit. Brother, the most welcome man to me, that the world holdeth !

Men. Tra. I joy, and ten thousand joys the more, having taken so long travel and huge pains to seek you.   119

Mess. See now, how all this matter comes about.   Thus it was that the gentlewoman had ye in to dinner, thinking it had been he.

Men. Cit. True it is I willed a dinner to be provided for me here this morning ; and I also brought hither closely a cloak of my wife's, and gave it to this woman.   125

Men. Tra. Is not this the same, brother ?

Men. Cit. How came you by this ?

Men. Tra. This woman met me ; had me in to dinner ; entertained me most kindly ; and gave me this cloak, and this chain.   130

Men. Cit. Indeed she took ye for me : and I believe I have been as strangely handled by occasion of your coming.

Mess. You shall have time enough to laugh at all these matters hereafter.   Do ye remember, master, what ye promised me ?   135

Men.[1] optumum atque aequissumum orat, frater : far caussa
mea.

Men.[2] liber esto.   *Men.*[1] quom tu es liber, gaudeo, Messenio.
Mes. sed meliorest opus auspicio, ut liber perpetuo siem.
Men.[2] quoniam haec euenere, frater, nostra | ex sententia, 90
in patriam redeamus ambo.   *Men.*[1] frater, faciam, ut tu uoles.
auctionem hic faciam et uendam quidquid est. nunc interim
eamus intro, frater.   *Men.*[2] fiat.   *Mes.* scitin quid ego uos
rogo.

Men.[1] quid ?   *Mes.* praeconium mi ut detis.   *Men.*[2] dabitur.
Mes. ergo nunciam
uis conclamari auctionem ?   *Men.*[1] fore quidem dieseptumi. 95
Mes. auctio fiet Menaechmi mane sane septumi.
uenibunt serui, supellex, fundi, aédes, omnia.
uenibunt quiqui licebunt, praesenti pecunia.
uenibit—uxor quoque etiam, si quis emptor uenerit.
uix credo tota auctione capiet quinquagesies.   100
nunc, spectatores, ualete et nobis clare plaudite.

FINIS

Men. Cit. Brother, I will entreat you to perform your promise to Messenio : he is worthy of it.

Men. Tra. I am content.

Mess. Io Triumphe !   139

Men. Tra. Brother, will ye now go with me to Syracusis ?

Men. Cit. So soon as I can sell away such goods as I possess here in Epidamnum, I will go with you.

Men. Tra. Thanks, my good brother.

Men. Cit. Messenio, play thou the crier for me, and make a proclamation.   145

Mess. A fit office.   Come on.   Oh yes !
What day shall your sale be ?

Men. Cit. This day sennight.   148

Mess. [cries] All men, women and children in Epidamnum, or elsewhere, that will repair to Menechmus' house this day sennight, shall there find all manner of things to sell ; servants, household stuff, house, ground and all ; so they bring ready money.   Will ye sell your wife too, sir ?

Men. Cit. Yea, but I think nobody will bid money for her.   155

Mess. Thus, gentlemen, we take our leaves, and if we have pleased, we require a Plaudite.

FINIS

NOTES

p. 14. *Peniculus :* 'a sponge,' 'a brush.'

p. 22, l. 49. 'Nay, further yet with a will from the lion's cave.'

'Good for ye! 'tis pity ye were not made a charioteer to drive in a race,' who had to look behind for fear of a foul from his competitors.

p. 24, l. 1. 'I don't count you.' 'Then I am in the same case as the adscriptivi,' who were enrolled as reserves to fill the places of the killed : not on the strength of the regiment. Until a soldier was *in numeris*, he was not officially *miles*.

Below, the translator takes *tua est legio* as 'the legion is under your command.' Is it possible that *legio* is used in its original sense of choice ?

'Drink for the heavens' I do not understand. The old texts read *pro Ilio :* perhaps the translator had *caelo* somewhere in his copy. He paraphrases freely here, however.

p. 26, l. 17. 'garter': girdle.

p. 26, l. 20. 'Thus . . . lovers' probably belongs to Erotium ; the next line to P. (aside).

'mary-bone': marrow-bone.

p. 27, l. 42. 'lese': lose.

p. 28, l. 3. M. says really that he would feel happier to see his own country again.

p. 32, l. 44 omitted in trans. ; the author here compresses.

p. 32, ll. 7, 8 are run into one by the old texts. The Ambr. shows that there were two : they seem to have run thus :

Men. Tra. A good day to you, whoever you are.

Cyl. Whoever I am ! What! don't you know who I am ?

Men. Tra. Not I, i' faith.

Cylindrus then continues : Where are the other guests ?

The first word of l. 8 is certainly *non*, not *noui*, as Fleckeisen conjectured.

The translation 'no, not I' must be taken ironically. Below,
ll. 12–13 are omitted; the Ambr. shows another lost line.

p. 33, l. 34. 'catchpoles, cony-catchers': constables, cheats.

p. 33, l. 39. *sine aamno:* without loss.

p. 34, l. 22. Culindrus should be read here, with a pun on
culleus (leather bag); Coriendrus, a pun on *corium* (leather).

p. 36, l. 36. *hicquidem:* he said I was mad, now I see he
is so.

p. 36, l. 51. 'Well, I'll go and see about dressing the
meat.'

p. 36, ll. 53–58 compressed.

p. 38, 1 ff. The speech is compressed; this is so often
done that it will not be noted after this except for some special
reason.

p. 45, l. 63. 'Pythia' should be Phintia.
(This succession is not in the history.)

p. 47, l. 84. 'dyers': worker in gold embroidery.

p. 47, l. 94. 'sot': fool.

p. 49, l. 95, 'Ay, master': there is nothing of this in the Latin
perii, "I'm done for."

p. 48, l. 1. Twenty: thirty.

p. 53, l. 39. Pediculus: the pun is not in the Latin, from
which the trans. here departs.

p. 54. *Ancilla* means Maid: it is not a proper name.
Act IV. *Mulier:* woman.

p. 60, ll. 19–21 are omitted.

p. 79. *Senex:* old man.

p. 82, ll. 51–2 are omitted, and the speech of Men. aside
inserted.

p. 91. *Medicus:* Physician.
The last speech of Men. Tra. comes after the first speech of Sen.;
the translator has compressed it.

p. 105, l. 41. *Servus alius:* another slave. He is not in the
original caste.

p. 109, l. 17. 'Whew . . .': not in text.

p. 113, l. 70. This quick dialogue is a paraphrase of a longer
speech of Messenio.

p. 119, l. 157. *Plaudite:* please applaud. This was the actors'
appeal at the end of a play.

CPSIA information can be obtained
at www.ICGtesting.com
Printed in the USA
BVHW052116120122
626036BV00008B/187

9 781164 006374